Website Scraping with Python

Using BeautifulSoup and Scrapy

Gábor László Hajba

Apress®

Website Scraping with Python

Gábor László Hajba
Sopron, Hungary

ISBN-13 (pbk): 978-1-4842-3924-7   ISBN-13 (electronic): 978-1-4842-3925-4
https://doi.org/10.1007/978-1-4842-3925-4

Library of Congress Control Number: 2018957273

Managing Director, Apress Media LLC: Welmoed Spahr
Acquisitions Editor: Todd Green
Development Editor: James Markham
Coordinating Editor: Jill Balzano

Cover designed by eStudioCalamar

Cover image designed by Freepik (www.freepik.com)

Distributed to the book trade worldwide by Springer Science+Business Media New York, 233 Spring Street, 6th Floor, New York, NY 10013. Phone 1-800-SPRINGER, fax (201) 348-4505, e-mail orders-ny@springer-sbm.com, or visit www.springeronline.com. Apress Media, LLC is a California LLC and the sole member (owner) is Springer Science + Business Media Finance Inc (SSBM Finance Inc). SSBM Finance Inc is a **Delaware** corporation.

For information on translations, please e-mail rights@apress.com, or visit www.apress.com/rights-permissions.

Apress titles may be purchased in bulk for academic, corporate, or promotional use. eBook versions and licenses are also available for most titles. For more information, reference our Print and eBook Bulk Sales web page at www.apress.com/bulk-sales.

Any source code or other supplementary material referenced by the author in this book is available to readers on GitHub via the book's product page, located at www.apress.com/9781484239247. For more detailed information, please visit http://www.apress.com/source-code.

Printed on acid-free paper

To those who are restless, like me,
and always want to learn something new.

Table of Contents

About the Author

Gábor László Hajba is a Senior Consultant at EBCONT enterprise technologies, who specializes in Java, Python, and Crystal. He is responsible for designing and developing customer needs in the enterprise software world. He has also held roles as an Advanced Software Engineer with Zühlke Engineering, and as a freelance developer with Porsche Informatik. He considers himself a workaholic, (hard)core and well-grounded developer, pragmatic minded, and freak of portable apps and functional code.

He currently resides in Sopron, Hungary with his loving wife, Ágnes.

About the Technical Reviewer

 **Chaim Krause** is an expert computer programmer with over thirty years of experience to prove it. He has worked as a lead tech support engineer for ISPs as early as 1995, as a senior developer support engineer with Borland for Delphi, and has worked in Silicon Valley for over a decade in various roles, including technical support engineer and developer support engineer. He is currently a military simulation specialist for the US Army's Command and General Staff College, working on projects such as developing serious games for use in training exercises.

He has also authored several video training courses on Linux topics and has been a technical reviewer for over twenty books, including iOS Code Testing, Android Apps for Absolute Beginners (4ed), and XML Essentials for C# and .NET Development (all Apress). It seems only natural then that he would be an avid gamer and have his own electronics lab and server room in his basement. He currently resides in Leavenworth, Kansas with his loving partner, Ivana, and a menagerie of four-legged companions: their two dogs, Dasher and Minnie, and their three cats, Pudems, Talyn, and Alaska.

Acknowledgments

Many people have contributed to what is good in this book. Remaining errors and problems are the author's alone.

Thanks to Apress for making this book happen. Without them, I'd have never considered approaching a publisher with my book idea.

Thanks to the editors, especially Jill Balzano and James Markham. Their advices made this book much better.

Thanks to Chaim Krause, who pointed out missing technical information that may be obvious to me but not for the readers.

Last but not least, a big thank you to my wife, Ágnes, for enduring the time invested in this book.

I hope this book will be a good resource to get your own website scraping projects started!

Introduction

Welcome to our journey together exploring website scraping solutions using the Python programming language!

As the title already tells you, this book is about website scraping with Python. I distilled my knowledge into this book to give you a useful manual if you want to start data gathering from websites.

Website scraping is (in my opinion) an emerging topic.

I expect you have Python programming knowledge. This means I won't clarify every code block I write or constructs I use. But because of this, you're allowed to differ: every programmer has his/her own unique coding style, and your coding results can be different than mine.

This book is split into six chapters:

1. **Getting Started** is to get you started with this book: you can learn what website scraping is and why it worth writing a book about this topic.

2. **Enter the Requirements** introduces the requirements we will use to implement website scrapers in the follow-up chapters.

3. **Using Beautiful Soup** introduces you to Beautiful Soup, an HTML content parser that you can use to write website scraper scripts. We will implement a scraper to gather the requirements of Chapter 2 using Beautiful Soup.

4. **Using Scrapy** introduces you to Scrapy, the (in my opinion) best website scraping toolbox available for the Python programming language. We will use Scrapy to implement a website scraper to gather the requirements of Chapter 2.

5. **Handling JavaScript** shows you options for how you can deal with websites that utilize JavaScript to load data dynamically and through this, give users a better experience. Unfortunately, this makes basic website scraping a torture but there are options that you can rely on.

6. **Website Scraping in the Cloud** moves your scrapers from running on your computer locally to remote computers in the Cloud. I'll show you free and paid providers where you can deploy your spiders and automate the scraping schedules.

You can read this book from cover to cover if you want to learn the different approaches of website scraping with Python. If you're interested only in a specific topic, like Scrapy for example, you can jump straight to Chapter 4, although I recommend reading Chapter 2 because it contains the description of the data gathering task we will implement in the vast part of the book.

CHAPTER 1

Getting Started

Instead of installation instructions, which follow later for each library, we will dive right into deep water: this chapter introduces website scraping in general and the requirements we will implement throughout this book.

You may expect a thorough introduction into website scraping, but because you are reading this book I expect you already know what website scraping is and you want to learn how to do it with Python.

Therefore, I'll just give you a glance at the topic and jump right into the depths of creating a script that scrapes websites!

Website Scraping

The need to scrape websites came with the popularity of the Internet, where you share your content and a lot of data. The first widely known scrapers were invented by search engine developers (like Google or AltaVista). These scrapers go through (almost) the whole Internet, scan every web page, extract information from it, and build an index that you can search.

Everyone can create a scraper. Few of us will try to implement such a big application, which could be new competition to Google or Bing. But we can narrow the scope to one or two web pages and extract information in a structured manner–and get the results exported to a database or structured file (JSON, CSV, XML, Excel sheets).

© Gábor László Hajba 2018
G. L. Hajba, *Website Scraping with Python*, https://doi.org/10.1007/978-1-4842-3925-4_1

Nowadays, *digital transformation* is the new buzzword companies use and want to engage. One component of this transformation is providing data access points to everyone (or at least to other companies interested in that data) through APIs. With those APIs available, you do not need to invest time and other resources to create a website scraper.

Even though providing APIs is something scraper developers won't benefit from, the process is slow, and many companies don't bother creating those access points because they have a website and it is enough to maintain.

Projects for Website Scraping

There are a lot of use cases where you can leverage your knowledge of website scraping. Some might be common sense, while others are extreme cases. In this section you will find some use cases where you can leverage your knowledge.

The main reason to create a scraper is to extract information from a website. This information can be a list of products sold by a company, nutrition details of groceries, or NFL results from the last 15 years. Most of these projects are the groundwork for further data analysis: gathering all this data manually is a long and error-prone process.

Sometimes you encounter projects where you need to extract data from one website to load it into another–a migration. I recently had a project where my customer moved his website to WordPress and the old blog engine's export functionality wasn't meant to import it into WordPress. I created a scraper that extracted all the posts (around 35,000) with their images, did some formatting on the contents to use WordPress short codes, and then imported all those posts into the new website.

A weird project could be to download the whole Internet! Theoretically it is not impossible: you start at a website, download it, extract and follow all the links on this page, and download the new sites too. If the websites you scrape all have links to each other, you can browse (and download) the whole Internet. I don't suggest you start this project because you won't have enough disk space to contain the entire Internet, but the idea is interesting. Let me know how far you reached if you implement a scraper like this.

Websites Are the Bottleneck

One of the most difficult parts of gathering data through websites is that websites differ. I mean not only the data but the layout too. It is hard to create a good-fit-for-all scraper because every website has a different layout, uses different (or no) HTML IDs to identify fields, and so on.

And if this is not enough, many websites change their layout frequently. If this happens, your scraper is not working as it did previously. In these cases, the only option is to revisit your code and adapt it to the changes of the target website.

Unfortunately, you won't learn secret tricks that will help you create a scraper that always works–if you want to write specialized data extractors. I will show some examples in this book that will always work if the HTML standard is in use.

Tools in This Book

In this book you will learn the basic tools you can use in Python to do your website scraping. You will soon realize how hard it is to create every single piece of a scraper from scratch.

But Python has a great community, and a lot of projects are available to help you focus on the important part of your scraper: data extraction. I will introduce you to tools like the `requests` library, `Beautiful Soup`, and `Scrapy`.

The `requests` library is a lightweight wrapper over the tedious task of handling HTTP, and it emerged as the recommended way:

> *The Requests package is recommended for a higher level HTTP client interface.*

> — Python 3 documentation

`Beautiful Soup` is a content parser. It is not a tool for website scraping because it doesn't navigate pages automatically and it is hard to scale. But it aids in parsing content, and gives you options to extract the required information from XML and HTML structures in a friendly manner.

`Scrapy` is a website scraping framework/library. It is much more powerful than `Beautiful Soup`, and it can be scaled. Therefore, you can create more complex scrapers easier with `Scrapy`. But on the other side, you have more options to configure. Fine-tuning `Scrapy` can be a problem, and you can mess up a lot if you do something wrong. But with great power comes great responsibility: you must use `Scrapy` with care.

Even though `Scrapy` is **the Python library** created for website scraping, sometimes I just prefer a combination of `requests` and `Beautiful Soup` because it is lightweight, and I can write my scraper in a short period–and I do not need scaling or parallel execution.

Preparation

When starting a website scraper, even if it is a small script, you must prepare yourself for the task. There are some legal and technical considerations for you right at the beginning.

In this section I will give you a short list of what you should do to be prepared for a website scraping job or task:

1. Do the website's owners allow scraping? To find out, read the *Terms & Conditions* and the *Privacy Policy* of the website.

4

2. Can you scrape the parts you are interested in? See the `robots.txt` file for more information and use a tool that can handle this information.

3. What technology does the website use? There are free tools available that can help you with this task, but you can look at the website's HTML code to find out.

4. What tools should I use? Depending on your task and the website's structure, there are different paths you can choose from.

Now let's see a detailed description for each item mentioned.

Terms and Robots

Scraping currently has barely any limitations; there are no laws defining what can be scraped and what cannot.

However, there are guidelines that define what you should respect. There is no enforcing; you can completely ignore these recommendations, but you shouldn't.

Before you start any scraping task, look at the *Terms & Conditions* and *Privacy Policy* of the website you want to gather data from. If there is no limitation on scraping, then you should look at the `robots.txt` file for the given website(s).

When reading the terms and conditions of a website, you can search for following keywords to find restrictions:

- scraper/scraping
- crawler/crawling
- bot
- spider
- program

Most of the time these keywords can be found, and this makes your search easier. If you have no luck, you need to read through the whole legal content and it is not as easy—at least I think legal stuff is always dry to read.

In the European Union there's a data protection right that has been live for some years but strictly enforced from 2018: GDPR. Keep the private data of private persons out of your scraping—you can be held liable if some of it slips out into public because of your scraper.

---

robots.txt

Most websites provide a file called robots.txt, which is used to tell web crawlers what they can scrape and what they should not touch. Naturally, it is up to the developer to respect these recommendations, but I advise you to **always obey** the contents of the robots.txt file.

Let's see one example of such a file:

```
User-agent: *
Disallow: /covers/
Disallow: /api/
Disallow: /*checkval
Disallow: /*wicket:interface
Disallow: ?print_view=true
Disallow: /*/search
Disallow: /*/product-search
Allow: /*/product-search/discipline
Disallow: /*/product-search/discipline?*facet-subj=
Disallow: /*/product-search/discipline?*facet-pdate=
Disallow: /*/product-search/discipline?*facet-type=category
```

The preceding code block is from www.apress.com/robots.txt. As you can see, most content tells what is disallowed. For example, scrapers shouldn't scrape www.apress.com/covers/.

Besides the Allow and Disallow entries, the User-agent can be interesting. Every scraper should have an identification, which is provided through the user agent parameter. Bigger bots, created by Google and Bing, have their unique identifier. And because they are scrapers that add your pages to the search results, you can define *excludes* for these bots to leave you alone. Later in this chapter, you will create a script which will examine and follow the guidelines of the robots.txt file with a custom user agent.

There can be other entries in a robots.txt file, but they are not standard. To find out more about those entries, visit https://en.wikipedia.org/wiki/Robots_exclusion_standard.

Technology of the Website

Another useful preparation step is to look at the technologies the targeted website uses.

There is a Python library called builtwith, which aims to detect the technologies a website utilizes. The problem with this library is that the last version *1.3.2* was released in 2015, and it is not compatible with Python 3. Therefore, you cannot use it as you do with libraries available from the PyPI.[1]

However, in May 2017, Python 3 support has been added to the sources, but the new version was not released (yet, I'm writing this in November 2017). This doesn't mean we cannot use the tool; we must manually install it.

First, download the sources from https://bitbucket.org/richardpenman/builtwith/downloads/. If you prefer, you can clone the repository with Mercurial to stay up to date if new changes occur.

After downloading the sources, navigate to the folder where you downloaded the sources and execute the following command:

```
pip install .
```

---

[1]PyPI – the Python Package Index

The command installs builtwith to your Python environment and you can use it.

Now if you open a Python CLI, you can look at your target site to see what technologies it uses.

```
>>> from builtwith import builtwith
>>> builtwith('http://www.apress.com')
{'javascript-frameworks': ['AngularJS', 'jQuery'],
'font-scripts': ['Font Awesome'], 'tag-managers':
['Google Tag Manager'], 'analytics': ['Optimizely']}
```

The preceding code block shows which technologies Apress uses for its website. You can learn from AngularJS that if you plan to write a scraper, you should be prepared to handle dynamic content that is rendered with JavaScript.

builtwith is not a magic tool, it is a website scraper that downloads the given URL; parses its contents; and based on its knowledge base, it tells you which technologies the website uses. This tool uses basic Python features, which means sometimes you cannot get information in the website you are interested in, but most of the time you get enough information.

Using Chrome Developer Tools

To walk through the website and identify the fields of the requirements, we will use Google Chrome's built-in *DevTools*. If you do not know what this tool can do for you, here is a quick introduction.

The Chrome Developer Tools (DevTools for short), are a set of web authoring and debugging tools built into Google Chrome. The DevTools provide web developers deep access into the internals of the browser and their web application. Use the DevTools to efficiently track down layout issues, set JavaScript breakpoints, and get insights for code optimization.

As you can see, DevTools give you tools to see inside the workings of the browser. We don't need anything special; we will use DevTools to see where the information resides.

In this section I will guide us with screenshots through the steps I usually do when I start (or just evaluate) a scraping project.

Set-up

First, you must prepare to get the information. Even though we know which website to scrape and what kind of data to extract, we need some preparation.

Basic website scrapers are simple tools that download the contents of the website into memory and then do extraction on this data. This means they are not capable of running dynamic content just like JavaScript, and therefore we have to make our browser similar to a simple scraper by disabling JavaScript rendering.

First, right-click with your mouse on the web page and from the menu select "Inspect," as shown in Figure 1-1.

Back	Alt+Left Arrow
Forward	Alt+Right Arrow
Reload	Ctrl+R
Save as...	Ctrl+S
Print...	Ctrl+P
Cast...	
Translate to English	
View page source	Ctrl+U
Inspect	Ctrl+Shift+I

Figure 1-1. *Starting Chrome's DevTools*

Alternatively, you can press CTRL+SHIFT+I in Windows or ⌘+⇧+I on a Mac to open the DevTools window.

Then locate the settings button (the three vertically aligned dots, as shown in Figure 1-2.) and click it:

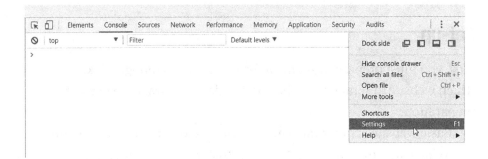

Figure 1-2. *The Settings menu is located under the three dots*

Alternatively, you can press F1 in Windows.

Now scroll down to the bottom of the *Settings* screen and make sure Disable JavaScript is checked, as shown in Figure 1-3.

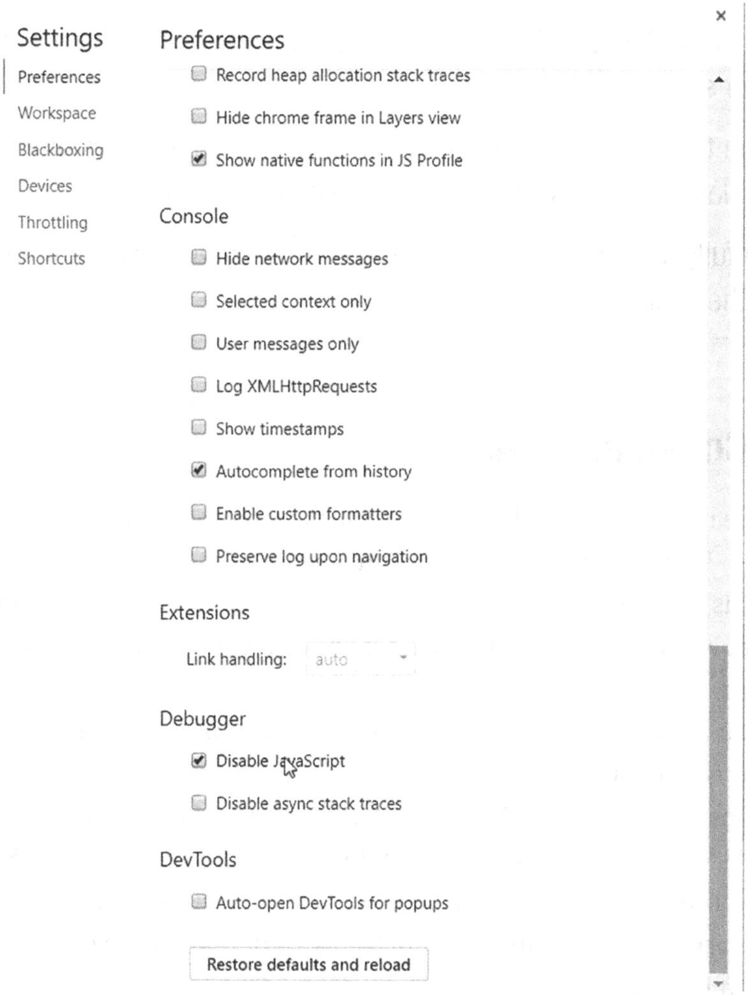

Settings   Preferences

Preferences   ☐ Record heap allocation stack traces

Workspace   ☐ Hide chrome frame in Layers view

Blackboxing   ☑ Show native functions in JS Profile

Devices

Throttling   Console

Shortcuts   ☐ Hide network messages

                    ☐ Selected context only

                    ☐ User messages only

                    ☐ Log XMLHttpRequests

                    ☐ Show timestamps

                    ☑ Autocomplete from history

                    ☐ Enable custom formatters

                    ☐ Preserve log upon navigation

                    Extensions

                    Link handling: auto   ▼

                    Debugger

                    ☑ Disable JavaScript

                    ☐ Disable async stack traces

                    DevTools

                    ☐ Auto-open DevTools for popups

                    [Restore defaults and reload]

Figure 1-3. *Disabling JavaScript*

Now reload the page, exit the *Settings* window, but stay in the inspector view because we will use the HTML element selector available here.

Note   Disabling JavaScript is necessary if you want to see how your scraper sees the website.

Later in this book, you will learn options how to scrape websites that utilize JavaScript to render dynamic content.

But to fully understand and enjoy those extra capabilities, you must learn the basics.

Tool Considerations

If you are reading this book, you will write your scrapers most likely with Python 3. However, you must decide on which tools to use.

In this book you will learn the tools of the trade and you can decide on your own what to use, but now I'll share with you how I decide on an approach.

If you are dealing with a simple website–and by simple, I mean one that is not using JavaScript excessively for rendering–then you can choose between creating a crawler with Beautiful Soup + requests or use Scrapy. If you must deal with a lot of data and want to speed things up, use Scrapy. In the end, you will use Scrapy in 90% of your tasks, and you can integrate Beautiful Soup into Scrapy and use them together.

If the website uses JavaScript for rendering, you can either reverse engineer the AJAX/XHR calls and use your preferred tool, or you can reach out to a tool that renders websites for you. Such tools are Selenium and Portia. I will introduce you to these approaches in this book and you can decide which fits you best, which is easier for you to use.

Starting to Code

After this lengthy introduction, it is time to write some code. I guess you are keen to get your fingers "dirty" and create your first scrapers.

In this section we will write simple Python 3 scripts to get you started with scraping and to utilize some of the information you read previously in this chapter.

These miniscripts won't be full-fledged applications, just small demos of what is awaiting you in this book.

Parsing robots.txt

Let's create an application that parses the robots.txt file of the target website and acts based on the contents.

Python has a built-in module that is called robotparser, which enables us to read and understand the robots.txt file and ask the parser if we can scrape a given part of the target website.

We will use the previously shown robots.txt file from Apress.com. To follow along, open your Python editor of choice, create a file called robots.py, and add the following code:

```python
from urllib import robotparser

robot_parser = robotparser.RobotFileParser()

def prepare(robots_txt_url):
    robot_parser.set_url(robots_txt_url)
    robot_parser.read()

def is_allowed(target_url, user_agent='*'):
    return robot_parser.can_fetch(user_agent, target_url)
```

```
if __name__ == '__main__':
    prepare('http://www.apress.com/robots.txt')

    print(is_allowed('http://www.apress.com/covers/'))
    print(is_allowed('http://www.apress.com/gp/python'))
```

Now let's run the example application. If we have done everything right (and Apress didn't change its robot guidelines), we should get back False and True, because we are not allowed to access the covers folder, but there is no restriction on the Python section.

```
> python robots.py
False
True
```

This code snippet is good if you write your own scraper and you don't use Scrapy. Integrating the robotparser and checking every URL before accessing it helps you automate the task of honoring the website owners' request what to access.

Previously, in this chapter, I mentioned that you can define user agent–specific restrictions in a robots.txt file. Because I have no access to the Apress website, I created a custom entry on my own homepage for this book and this entry looks like this:

```
User-Agent: bookbot
Disallow: /category/software-development/java-software-
development/
```

Now to see how this works. For this, you must modify the previously written Python code (robots.py) or create a new one to provide a user agent when you call the is_allowed function because it already accepts a user agent as argument.

```
from urllib import robotparser

robot_parser = robotparser.RobotFileParser()
```

```python
def prepare(robots_txt_url):
    robot_parser.set_url(robots_txt_url)
    robot_parser.read()

def is_allowed(target_url, user_agent='*'):
    return robot_parser.can_fetch(user_agent, target_url)

if __name__ == '__main__':
    prepare('http://hajba.hu/robots.txt')

    print(is_allowed('http://hajba.hu/category/software-
development/java-software-development/', 'bookbot'))
    print(is_allowed('http://hajba.hu/category/software-
development/java-software-development/', 'my-agent'))
    print(is_allowed('http://hajba.hu/category/software-
development/java-software-development/', 'googlebot'))
```

The preceding code will result in the following output:

```
False
True
True
```

Unfortunately, you cannot prevent malicious bots from scraping your website because in most cases they will ignore the settings in your robots.txt file.

Creating a Link Extractor

After this lengthy introduction, it is time to create our first scraper, which will extract links from a given page.

This example will be simple; we won't use any specialized tools for website scraping, just libraries available with the standard Python 3 installation.

Let's open a text editor (or the Python IDE of your choice). We will work in a file called link_extractor.py.

```python
from urllib.request import urlopen
import re

def download_page(url):
    return urlopen(url).read().decode('utf-8')

def extract_links(page):
    link_regex = re.compile('<a[^>]+href=["\'](.*?)["\']',
    re.IGNORECASE)
    return link_regex.findall(page)

if __name__ == '__main__':
    target_url = 'http://www.apress.com/'
    apress = download_page(target_url)
    links = extract_links(apress)

    for link in links:
        print(link)
```

The preceding code block extracts all the links, which you can find at the Apress homepage (on the first page only). If you run the code with the Python command link_extractor.py, you will see a lot of URLs that start with a slash (/) without any domain information. This is because those are internal links on the apress.com website. To fix this, we could manually look for such entries in the links set, or use a tool already present in the Python standard library: urljoin.

```python
from urllib.request import urlopen, urljoin
import re

def download_page(url):
    return urlopen(url).read().decode('utf-8')
```

```
def extract_links(page):
    link_regex = re.compile('<a[^>]+href=["\'](.*?)["\']',
    re.IGNORECASE)
    return link_regex.findall(page)

if __name__ == '__main__':
    target_url = 'http://www.apress.com/'
    apress = download_page(target_url)
    links = extract_links(apress)

    for link in links:
        print(urljoin(target_url, link))
```

As you can see, when you run the modified code, this new method adds http://www.apress.com to every URL that is missing this prefix, for example http://www.apress.com/gp/python, but leaves others like https://twitter.com/apress intact.

The previous code example uses regular expressions to find all the anchor tags (<a>) in the HTML code of the website. Regular expressions are a hard topic to learn, and they are not easy to write. That's why we won't dive deeper into this topic and will use more high-level tools, like Beautiful Soup, in this book to extract our contents.

Extracting Images

In this section we will extract image sources from the website. We won't download any images yet, just lay hands on the information about where these images are in the web.

Images are very similar to links from the previous section, but they are defined by the <img> tag and have a src attribute instead of an href.

With this information you can stop here and try to write the extractor on your own. Following, you'll find my solution.

```
from urllib.request import urlopen, urljoin
import re

def download_page(url):
    return urlopen(url).read().decode('utf-8')

def extract_image_locations(page):
    img_regex = re.compile('<img[^>]+src=["\'](.*?)["\']',
    re.IGNORECASE)
    return img_regex.findall(page)

if __name__ == '__main__':
    target_url = 'http://www.apress.com/'
    apress = download_page(target_url)
    image_locations = extract_image_locations(apress)

    for src in image_locations:
        print(urljoin(target_url, src))
```

If you take a close look, I modified just some variable names and the regular expression. I could have used the link extractor from the previous section and changed only the expression.

Summary

In this chapter you've gotten a basic introduction to website scraping and how to prepare for a scraping job.

Besides the introduction, you created your first building blocks for scrapers that extracted information from a web page, like links and image sources.

As you may guess, Chapter 1 was just the beginning. There is a lot more coming up in the following chapters.

You will learn the requirements for which you must create a scraper, and you will write your first scrapers using tools like Beautiful Soup and Scrapy. Stay tuned and continue reading!

CHAPTER 2

Enter the Requirements

After the introductory chapter, it is time to get you started with a real scraping project.

In this chapter you will learn what data you must extract throughout the next two chapters, using Beautiful Soup and Scrapy.

Don't worry; the requirements are simple. We will extract information from the following website: https://www.sainsburys.co.uk/.

Sainsbury's is an online shop with a lot of goods provided. This makes a great source for a website scraping project.

I'll guide you to find your way to the requirements, and you'll learn how I approach a scraping project.

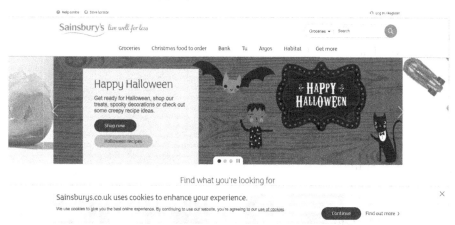

Figure 2-1. *The landing page of Sainsbury's at Halloween 2017*

© Gábor László Hajba 2018
G. L. Hajba, *Website Scraping with Python*, https://doi.org/10.1007/978-1-4842-3925-4_2

The Requirements

If you look at the website, you can see this is a simple web page with a lot of information. Let me show you which parts we will extract.

One idea would be to extract something from the Halloween-themed site (see Figure 2-1. for their themed landing page). However, this is not an option because you cannot try this yourself; Halloween is over when you read this–at least for 2017, and I cannot guarantee that the future sales will be the same.

Therefore, you will extract information on groceries. To be more specific, you will gather nutrition details from the "Meat & fish" department.

For every entry, which has nutrition details, you extract the following information:

- Name of the product

- URL of the product

- Item code

- Nutrition details per 100g:

  - Energy in kilocalories

  - Energy in kilojoules

  - Fat

  - Saturates

  - Carbohydrates

  - Total sugars

  - Starch

  - Fibre

  - Protein

  - Salt

- Country of origin

- Price per unit

- Unit

- Number of reviews

- Average rating

This looks like a lot, but do not worry! You will learn how to extract this information from **all** the products of this department with an automated script. And if you are keen and motivated, you can extend this knowledge and extract all the nutrition information for all the products.

Preparation

As I mentioned in the previous chapter, before you start your scraper development, you should look at the website's terms and conditions, and the robots.txt file to see if you can extract the information you need.

When writing this part (November 2017), there was no entry on scraper restrictions in the terms and conditions of the website. This means, you can create a bot to extract information.

The next step is to look at the robots.txt file, found at http://sainsburys.co.uk/robots.txt.

```
# __PUBLIC_IP_ADDR__   - Internet facing IP Address or
Domain name.
User-agent: *
Disallow: /webapp/wcs/stores/servlet/OrderItemAdd
Disallow: /webapp/wcs/stores/servlet/OrderItemDisplay
Disallow: /webapp/wcs/stores/servlet/OrderCalculate
Disallow: /webapp/wcs/stores/servlet/QuickOrderCmd
Disallow: /webapp/wcs/stores/servlet/InterestItemDisplay
```

```
Disallow: /webapp/wcs/stores/servlet/ProductDisplayLargeImageView
Disallow: /webapp/wcs/stores/servlet/QuickRegistrationFormView
Disallow: /webapp/wcs/stores/servlet/UserRegistrationAdd
Disallow: /webapp/wcs/stores/servlet/
          PostCodeCheckBeforeAddToTrolleyView
Disallow: /webapp/wcs/stores/servlet/Logon
Disallow: /webapp/wcs/stores/servlet/
          RecipesTextSearchDisplayView
Disallow: /webapp/wcs/stores/servlet/PostcodeCheckView
Disallow: /webapp/wcs/stores/servlet/ShoppingListDisplay
Disallow: /webapp/wcs/stores/servlet/gb/groceries/get-ideas/
          advertising
Disallow: /webapp/wcs/stores/servlet/gb/groceries/get-ideas/
          development
Disallow: /webapp/wcs/stores/servlet/gb/groceries/get-ideas/
          dormant
Disallow: /shop/gb/groceries/get-ideas/dormant/
Disallow: /shop/gb/groceries/get-ideas/advertising/
Disallow: /shop/gb/groceries/get-ideas/development

Sitemap: http://www.sainsburys.co.uk/sitemap.xml
```

In the code block you can see what is allowed and what is not, and this robots.txt is quite restrictive and has only Disallow entries but this is for all bots.

What can we find out from this text? For example, you shouldn't create bots that order automatically through this website. But this is unimportant for us because we only need to gather information—no purchasing. This robots.txt file has no limitations on our purposes; we are free to continue our preparation and scraping.

What would limit our purposes?   Good question. An entry in the robots.txt referencing the "Meat & fish" department could limit our scraping intent. A sample entry would look like this:

```
User-agent: *
Disallow: /shop/gb/groceries/meat-fish/
Disallow: /shop/gb/groceries/
```

But this won't allow search engines to look up the goods Sainsbury's is selling, and that would be a big profit loss.

Navigating Through "Meat & fishFish"

As mentioned at the beginning of this chapter, we will extract data from the "Meat & fish" department. The URL of this part of the website is www.sainsburys.co.uk/shop/gb/groceries/meat-fish.

Let's open the URL in our Chrome browser, disable JavaScript, and reload the browser window as described in the previous chapter. Remember, disabling JavaScript enables you to see the website's HTML code as a basic scraper will see it.

While I am writing this, the website of the department looks like Figure 2-2.

Figure 2-2. *The "Meat & fish" department's page inspected with Chrome's DevTools*

For our purposes, the navigation menu on the left side is interesting. It contains the links to the pages where we will find products to extract. Let's use the selection tool (or hit CTRL-SHIFT-C) and select the box containing these links, as shown in Figure 2-3.

Figure 2-3. *Selecting the navigation bar on the left*

Now we can see in the DevTools that every link is in a list element (`<li>` tag) of an unordered list (`<ul>`), with class `categories departments`. Note down this information because we will use it later.

Links, which have a little arrow pointing to the right (>), tell us they are just a grouping category and we will find another navigation menu beneath them if we click them. Let's examine the *Roast dinner* option, as shown in Figure 2-4.

Top sellers		Beef
Roast dinner	>	Chicken
Chicken & turkey	>	Duck
Beef	>	Gammon
Fish & seafood	>	Lamb
Bacon & sausages	>	Pork
Ham, deli meats & dips	>	Gravy & sauce
Pork & gammon	>	Yorkshire puds, stuffing & sides
Mince		Vegetables
Lamb	>	
Duck, game & venison		
Ready to cook	>	
Taste the Difference & organic	>	

Figure 2-4. *The "Roast dinner" submenu*

Here we can see that the page has no products but another list with links to detailed sites. If we look at the HTML structure in DevTools, we can see that these links are again elements of an unordered list. This unordered list has the class `categories aisles`.

Now we can go further into the *Beef* category, and here we have products listed (after a big filter box), as shown in Figure 2-5.

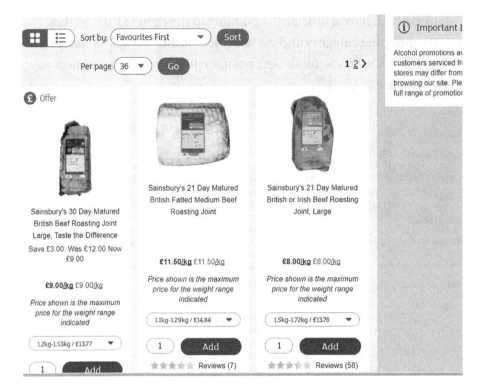

Figure 2-5. *Products in the "Beef" category*

Here we need to examine two things: one is the list of products; the other is the navigation.

If the category contains more products than 36 (this is the default count to show on the website), the items will be split into multiple pages. Because we want to extract information on all products, we must navigate through all those pages. If we select the navigation, we can see it is again an unordered list of the class pages, as shown in Figure 2-6.

```
                  .............._.._......_p.._g....._.............-.....--..-...g....,....p..,
         method="get">…</form>
       ▼<ul class="pages"> == $0
         ▶<li class="previous">…</li>
         ▶<li class="current">…</li>
         ▶<li>…</li>
       ▼<li class="next">
           ▶<a href="https://www.sainsburys.co.uk/shop/CategoryDisplay?
           pageSize=36&searchTe…
           stId=&categoryId=289463&langId=44&beginIndex=36&storeId=10151&
           promotionId=">…</a>
         </li>
       </ul>
```

Figure 2-6. *Unordered list with the class "pages"*

From those list elements, we are interested in the one with the right-pointing arrow symbol, which has the class next. This tells us if we have a next page we must navigate to or not.

Now let's find the link to the detail page of the products. All the products are in an unordered list (again). This list has the class productLister gridView, as shown in Figure 2-7.

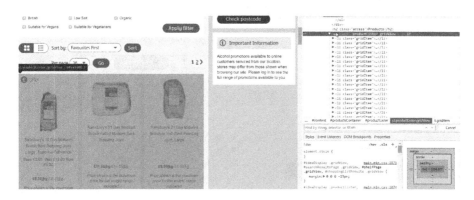

Figure 2-7. *Selecting the product list from the DevTools*

Every product is in a list element with the class gridItem. If we open up the details of one of those products we can see where the navigation link is: located in some divs and an h3. We note that the last div has the class productNameAndPromotions, as shown in Figure 2-8.

Figure 2-8. *Selecting the product's name*

Now we reached the level of the products, and we can step further and concentrate on the real task: identifying the required information.

Selecting the Required Information

We will discover the elements where our required information resides, based on the product shown in Figure 2-9.

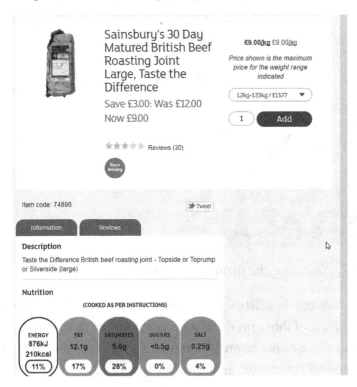

Figure 2-9. *The detailed product page we will use for the example*

Now that we have the product, let's identify the required information. As previously, we can use the select tool, locate the required text, and read the properties from the HTML code.

The **name** of the product is inside a header (h1), which is inside a div with the class productTitleDescriptionContainer.

The **price** and the **unit** are in a div of the class pricing. The price itself is in a paragraph (p) of the class pricePerUnit; the unit is in a span of the class pricePerUnitUnit.

Extracting the **rating** is tricky because here we only see the stars for the rating, but we want the numeric rating itself. Let's look at the image's HTML definition, as shown in Figure 2-10.

Figure 2-10. *The image's HTML code*

We can see the location of the image is inside a label of class numberOfReviews and it has an attribute, alt, which contains the decimal value of the averages of the reviews. After the image, there is the text containing the number of the reviews.

The **item code** is inside a paragraph of class itemCode.

29

The **nutrition information**, as shown in Figrue 2-11, is inside a `table` of class `nutritionTable`. Every row (`tr`) of this table contains one entry of our required data: the header (`th`) of the row has the name and the first column (`td`) contains the value. The only *exception* is the energy information, because two rows contain the values but only the first one the header. As you will see, we will solve this problem too with some specific code.

Table of Nutritional Information

(cooked as per instructions)	Per 100g	% based on RI for Average Adult
Energy	876kJ	-
	210kcal	11%
Fat	12.1g	17%
Saturates	5.6g	28%
Mono unsaturates	5.8g	-
Carbohydrate	<0.5g	-
Total Sugars	<0.5g	-
Fibre	<0.5g	-
Protein	25.2g	50%
Salt	0.25g	4%

RI= Reference Intakes of an average adult (8400kJ / 2000kcal)

Figure 2-11. *The nutrition table*

The country of origin, as shown in Figure 2-12, is inside a paragraph of a div of class `productText`. This field is not unique: every description is in a `productText  div`. This will make the extraction a bit complicated, but there is a solution for this too.

Figure 2-12. *Selecting the "Country of Origin" in Chrome's DevTools*

Even though we must extract many fields, we identified them easily in the website. Now it is time to extract the data and learn the tools of the trade!

Outlining the Application

After the requirements are defined and we've found each entry to extract, it is time to plan the applications structure and behavior.

If you think a bit about how to approach this project, you will start with big-bang, "Let's hammer the code" thinking. But you will realize later that you can break down the whole script into smaller steps. One example can be the following:

1. Download the starting page, in this case the "Meat & fish" department, and extract the links to the product pages.

2. Download the product pages and extract the links to the detailed products.

3. Extract the information we are interested in from the already downloaded product pages.

4. Export the extracted information.

And these steps could identify functions of the application we are developing.

31

Step **1** has a bit more to offer: if you remember the analysis with *DevTools* you have seen, some links are just a grouping category and you must extract the detail page links from this grouping category.

Navigating the Website

Before we jump into learning the first tools you will use to scrape website data, I want to show you how to navigate websites–and this will be another building block for scrapers.

Websites consist of pages and links between those pages. If you remember your mathematic studies, you will realize a website can be depicted as a graph, as shown in Figure 2-13.

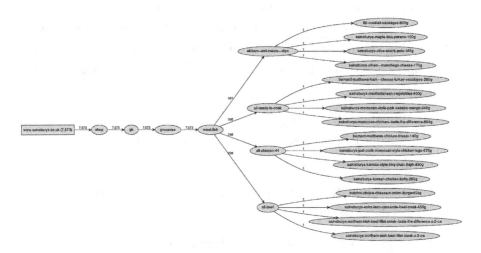

Figure 2-13. *The navigation path*

Because a website is a graph, you can use graph algorithms to navigate through the pages and links: Breadth First Search (BFS) and Depth First Search (DFS).

Using BFS, you go one level of the graph and gather all the URLs you need for the next level. For example, you start at the "Meat & fish" department page and extract all URLs to the next **required** level, like "*Top sellers*" or "*Roast dinner.*" Then you have all these URLs and go to the *Top sellers* and extract all URLs that lead to the detailed product pages. After this is done, you go to the "*Roast dinner*" page and extract all product details from there too, and so on. At the end you will have the URLs to all product pages, where you can go and extract the required information.

Using DFS, you go straight to the first product through "Meat & fish," "*Top sellers,*" and extract the information from its site. Then you go to the next product on the "*Top sellers*" page and extract the information from there. If you have all the products from "*Top sellers*" then you move to "*Roast dinner*" and extract all products from there.

If you ask me, both algorithms are good, and they deliver the same result. I could write two scripts and compare them to see which one is faster, but this comparison would be biased and flawed.[1]

Therefore, you will implement a script that will navigate a website, and you can change the algorithm behind it to use BFS or DFS.

If you are interested in the **Why?** for both algorithms, I suggest you consider Magnus Hetland's book: *Python Algorithms.*[2]

Creating the Navigation

Implementing the navigation is simple if you look at the algorithms, because this is the only trick: implement the pseudo code.

OK, I was a bit lazy, because you need to implement the link extraction too, which can be a bit complex, but you already have a building block from Chapter 1 and you are free to use it.

---

[1]Read more on this topic here: www.ibm.com/developerworks/library/
j-jtp02225/index.html

[2]www.apress.com/gp/book/9781484200568

```
def extract_links(page):
    if not page:
        return []
    link_regex = re.compile('<a[^>]+href=["\'](.*?)["\']',
    re.IGNORECASE)
    return [urljoin(page, link) for link in link_regex.
    findall(page)]

def get_links(page_url):
    host = urlparse(page_url)[1]
    page = download_page(page_url)
    links = extract_links(page)
    return [link for link in links if urlparse(link)[1] == host]
```

The two functions shown extract the page, and the links still point to the Sainsbury's website.

Note   If you don't filter out external URLs, your script may never end. This is only useful if you want to navigate the whole WWW to see how far you can reach from one website.

The extract_links function takes care of an empty or None page. urljoin wouldn't bleat about this but re.findall would throw an exception and you don't want that to happen.

The get_links function returns all the links of the web page that point to the same host. To find out which host to use, you can utilize the urlparse function,[3] which returns a tuple. The second parameter of this tuple is the host extracted from the URL.

---

[3]https://docs.python.org/3/library/urllib.parse.html

Those were the basics; now come the two search algorithms:

```python
def depth_first_search(start_url):
    from collections import deque
    visited = set()
    queue = deque()
    queue.append(start_url)
    while queue:
        url = queue.popleft()
        if url in visited:
            continue
        visited.add(url)
        for link in get_links(url):
            queue.appendleft(link)
        print(url)

def breadth_first_search(start_url):
    from collections import deque
    visited = set()
    queue = deque()
    queue.append(start_url)
    while queue:
        url = queue.popleft()
        if url in visited:
            continue
        visited.add(url)
        queue.extend(get_links(url))
        print(url)
```

If you look at the two functions just shown, you will see only one difference in their code (hint: it's highlighted): how you put them into the queue, which is a stack.

The **requests** Library

To implement the script successfully, you must learn a bit about the requests library.

I really like the extendedness of the Python core library, but sometimes you need libraries developed by members of the community. And the requests library is one of those.

With basic Python urlopen you can create simple requests and corresponding data, but it is complex to use. The requests library adds a friendly layer above this complexity and makes network programming easy: it takes care of redirects, and can handle sessions and cookies for you. The Python documentation recommends it as the tool to use.

Again, I won't give you a detailed introduction into this library, just the necessary information to get you going. If you need more information, look at the project's website.[4]

Installation

You, as a "Pythonista," already know how to install a library. But for the sake of completeness I include it here.

```
pip install requests
```

Now you are set up to continue this book.

Getting Pages

Requesting pages is easy with the requests library: `requests.get(url)`.

This returns a response object that contains basic information, like status code and content. The content is most often the body of the website you requested, but if you requested some binary data (like images or sound files) or JSON, then you get that back. For this book, we will focus on HTML content.

---

[4]Requests: HTTP for Humans: `http://docs.python-requests.org/en/master/`

You can get the HTML content from the response by calling its text parameter:

```
import requests
r = requests.get('http://www.hajba.hu')
if r.status_code == 200:
    print(r.text[:250])
else:
    print(r.status_code)
```

The preceding code block requests my website's front page, and if the server returns the status code 200, which means OK, it prints the first 250 characters of the content. If the server returns a different status, that code is printed.

You can see an example of a successful result as follows:

```
<!DOCTYPE html>
<html lang="en-US">
<head>

<meta property="og:type" content="website" />
<meta property="og:url" content="http://hajba.hu/2017/10/26/
red-hat-forum-osterreich-2017/" />
<meta name="twitter:card" content="summary_large_image" />
```

With this we are through the basics of the requests library. As I introduce more concepts of the library later in this book, I will tell you more about it.

Now it is time to skip the default urllib calls of Python 3 and change to requests.

Switching to requests

Now it is time to finish the script and use the requests library for downloading the pages.

By now you know already how to accomplish this, but here is the code anyway.

```
def download_page(url):
    try:
        return requests.get(url).text
    except:
        print('error in the url', url)
```

I surrounded the requesting method call with a try-except block because it can happen that the content has some encoding issues and we get an exception back that kills the whole application; and we don't want this because the website is big and starting over would require too much resources.[5]

Putting the Code Together

Now if you put everything together and run both functions with 'https://www.sainsburys.co.uk/shop/gb/groceries/meat-fish/' as starting_url, then you should get a similar result to this one.

starting navigation with BFS
```
https://www.sainsburys.co.uk/shop/gb/groceries/meat-fish/
http://www.sainsburys.co.uk
https://www.sainsburys.co.uk/shop/gb/groceries
https://www.sainsburys.co.uk/shop/gb/groceries/favourites
https://www.sainsburys.co.uk/shop/gb/groceries/great-offers
```

starting navigation with DFS
```
https://www.sainsburys.co.uk/shop/gb/groceries/meat-fish/
```

---

[5]I'll share a writing secret with you: I encountered six exceptions caused by encoding problems when I created the code for this chapter, and one was in the "Meat & fish" department.

```
http://www.sainsburys.co.uk/accessibility
http://www.sainsburys.co.uk/shop/gb/groceries
http://www.sainsburys.co.uk/terms
http://www.sainsburys.co.uk/cookies
```

If your result is slightly different, then the website's structure changed in the meantime.

As you can see from the printed URLs, the current solution is rudimentary: the code navigates the whole website instead of focusing only on the "Meat & fish" department and nutrition details.

One option would be to extend the filter to return only relevant links, but I don't like regular expressions because they are hard to read. Instead let's go ahead to the next chapter.

Summary

This chapter prepared you for the remaining parts of the book: you've met the requirements, analyzed the website to scrape, and identified where in the HTML code the fields of interest lay. And you implemented a simple scraper, mostly with basic Python tools, which navigates through the website.

In the next chapter you will learn Beautiful Soup, a simple extractor library that helps you to forget regular expressions, and adds more features to traverse and extract HTML-trees like a boss.

CHAPTER 3

Using Beautiful Soup

In this chapter, you will learn how to use Beautiful Soup, a lightweight Python library, to extract and navigate HTML content easily and forget overly complex regular expressions and text parsing.

Before I let you jump right into coding, I will tell you some things about this tool to familiarize yourself with it.

Feel free to jump to the next section if you are not in the mood for reading dry introductory text or basic tutorials; and if you don't understand something in my later approach or the code, come back here.

I find `Beautiful Soup` easy to use, and it is a perfect tool for handling HTML DOM elements: you can navigate, search, and even modify a document with this tool. It has a superb user experience, as you will see in the first section of this chapter.

Installing `Beautiful Soup`

Even though we both know you can install modules into your Python environment, for the sake of completeness let me (as always in this book) add a subsection for this trivial but mandatory task.

```
pip install beautifulsoup4
```

The number 4 is crucial because I developed and tested the examples in this book with version 4.6.0.

Simple Examples

After a lengthy introduction, it is time to start coding now, with simple examples to familiarize yourself with Beautiful Soup and try out some basic features without creating a complex scraper.

These examples will show the building blocks of Beautiful Soup and how to use them if needed.

You won't scrape an existing site, but instead will use HTML text prepared for each use case.

For these examples, I assume you've already entered from bs4 import BeautifulSoup into your Python script or interactive command line, so you have Beautiful Soup ready to use.

Parsing HTML Text

The very basic usage of Beautiful Soup, which you will see in every tutorial, is parsing and extracting information from an HTML string.

This is the basic step, because when you download a website, you send its content to Beautiful Soup to parse, but there is nothing to see if you pass a variable to the parser.

You will work most of the time with the following multiline string:

```
example_html = """
<html>
<head>
<title>Your Title Here</title>
</head>
<body bgcolor="#ffffff">
<center>
<img align="bottom" src="clouds.jpg"/>
</center>
<hr/>
```

```
<a href="http://somegreatsite.com">Link Name</a> is a link to
another nifty site
<h1>This is a Header</h1>
<h2>This is a Medium Header</h2>
Send me mail at <a href="mailto:support@yourcompany.
com">support@yourcompany.com</a>.
<p>This is a paragraph!</p>
<p>
<b>This is a new paragraph!</b><br/>
<b><i>This is a new sentence without a paragraph break, in bold
italics.</i></b>
<a>This is an empty anchor</a>
</p>
<hr/>
</body>
</html>
"""
```

To create a parse tree with Beautiful Soup, just write the following code:

```
soup = BeautifulSoup(example_html, 'html.parser')
```

The second argument to the function call defines which parser to use. If you don't provide any parser, you will get an error message like this:

```
UserWarning: No parser was explicitly specified, so I'm
using the best available HTML parser for this system
("html.parser"). This usually isn't a problem, but if you
run this code on another system, or in a different virtual
environment, it may use a different parser and behave
differently.
```

The code that caused this warning is on line 1 of the file
<stdin>. To get rid of this warning, change code that looks
like this:

```
BeautifulSoup(YOUR_MARKUP)
```

to this:

```
BeautifulSoup(YOUR_MARKUP, "html.parser")
```

This warning is well defined and tells you everything you need
to know. Because you can use different parsers with Beautiful Soup
(see later in this chapter), you cannot assume it will always use the same
parser; if a better one is installed, it will use that. Moreover, this can lead to
unexpected behavior, for example, your script slows down.

Now you can use the soup variable to navigate through the HTML.

Parsing Remote HTML

Beautiful Soup is not an HTTP client, so you cannot send URLs to it to do
extraction. You can try it out.

```
soup = BeautifulSoup('http://hajba.hu', 'html.parser')
```

The preceding code results in a warning message like this one:

```
UserWarning: "http://hajba.hu" looks like a URL. Beautiful Soup
is not an HTTP client. You should probably use an HTTP client
like requests to get the document behind the URL, and feed that
document to Beautiful Soup.
```

To convert remote HTML pages into a soup, you should use the
requests library.

```
soup = BeautifulSoup(requests.get('http://hajba.hu').text,
'html.parser')
```

Parsing a File

The third option to parse content is to read a file. You don't have to read the whole file; it is enough for Beautiful Soup if you provide an open file handle to its constructor and it does the rest.

```
with open('example.html') as infile:
    soup = BeautifulSoup(infile , 'html.parser')
```

Difference Between `find` and `find_all`

You will use two methods excessively with Beautiful Soup: find and find_all.

The difference between these two lies in their function and return type: find returns **only one**–if multiple nodes match the criteria, the first is returned; None, if nothing is found. find_all returns all results matching the provided arguments as a list; this list can be empty.

This means, every time you search for a tag with a certain id, you can use find because you can assume that an id is used only once in a page. Alternatively, if you are looking for the first occurrence of a tag, then you can use find too. If you are unsure, use find_all and iterate through the results.

Extracting All Links

The core function of a scraper is to extract links from the website that lead to other pages or other websites.

Links are in anchor tags (<a>), and where they point to is in the href attribute of these anchors. To find all anchor tags that have an href attribute, you can use following code:

```
links = soup.find_all('a', href=True)
for link in links:
    print(link['href'])
```

Running this code against the previously introduced HTML, you get the following result:

```
http://somegreatsite.com
mailto:support@yourcompany.com
```

The `find_all` method call includes the `href=True` argument. This tells `Beautiful Soup` to return only those anchor tags thaat have an `href` attribute. This gives you the freedom to access this attribute on resulting links without checking their existence.

To verify this, try running the preceding code, but remove the `href=True` argument from the function call. It results in an exception because the empty anchor doesn't have an `href` attribute.

You can add any attribute to the `find_all` method, and you can search for tags where the attribute is not present too.

Extracting All Images

The second biggest use case for scrapers is to extract images from websites and download them or just store their information, like where they are located, their display size, alternative text, and much more.

Like the link extractor, here you can use the `find_all` method of the soup, and specify filter tags.

```
images = soup.find_all('img', src=True)
```

Looking for a present `src` attribute helps to find images that have something to display. Naturally, sometimes the source attribute is added through JavaScript, and you must do some reverse engineering–but this is not the subject of this chapter.

Finding Tags Through Their Attributes

Sometimes you must find tags based on their attributes. For example, we identified HTML blocks for the requirements in the previous chapter through their class attribute.

The previous sections have shown you how to find tags where an attribute is present. Now it's time to find tags whose attributes have certain values.

Two use cases dominate this topic: searching by id or class attributes.

```
soup.find('p', id='first')
soup.find_all('p', class_='paragraph')
```

You can use any attribute in the find and find_all methods. The only exception is class because it is a keyword in Python. However, as you can see, you can use class_ instead.

This means you can search for images, where the source is clouds.jpg.

```
soup.find('img', src='clouds.jpg')
```

You can use regular expressions too to find tags that are of a specific type, and their attributes qualify them through some condition. For example, all image tags that display GIF files.

```
soup.find('img', src=re.compile('\.gif$'))
```

Moreover, the text of a tag is one of its attributes too. This means you can search for tags that contain a specific text (or just a fragment of a text).

```
soup.find_all('p', text='paragraph')
soup.find_all('p', text=re.compile('paragraph'))
```

The difference between the two preceding examples is their result. Because in the example HTML there is no paragraph that contains only the text "paragraph", an empty list is returned. The second method call returns a list of paragraph tags that contain the word "paragraph."

Finding Multiple Tags Based on Property

Previously, you have seen how to find one kind of tag (<p>, <img>) based on its properties.

47

However, Beautiful Soup offers you other options too: for example, you can find multiple tags that share the same criteria. Look at the next example:

```
for tag in soup.find_all(re.compile('h')):
    print(tag.name)
```

Here, you search for all tags that start with an h. The result would be something like this.

```
html
head
hr
h1
h2
hr
```

Another example would be to find all tags that contain the text "paragraph."

```
soup.find_all(True, text=re.compile('paragraph'))
```

Here you use the True keyword to match all tags. If you don't provide an attribute to narrow the search, you will get back a list of all tags in the HTML document.

Changing Content

I rarely use this function of Beautiful Soup, but valid use cases exist. Therefore I think you should learn about how to change the contents of a soup. Moreover, because I don't use this function a lot, this section is skinny and won't go into deep details.

Adding Tags and Attributes

Adding tags to the HTML is easy, though it is seldom used. If you add a tag, you must take care where and how you do it. You can use two methods: insert and append. Both work on a tag of the soup.

insert requires a position where to insert the new tag, and the new tag itself.

append requires only the new tag to append the new tag to the parent tag's end on which the method is called.

Because the soup itself is a tag, you can use these methods on it too, but you must take care. For example, try out the following code:

```
h2 = soup.new_tag('h2')
h2.string = 'This is a second-level header'
soup.insert(0, h2)
```

Here you want to insert the new tag, h2, into the soup at first place. This results in the following code (I omitted most of the HTML):

```
<h2>This is a second-level header</h2><html>
```

Alternatively, you can change the 0 to a 1, to insert the new tag at the second position. In this case, your tag is inserted at the end of the HTML, after the </html> tag.

```
soup.insert(1, h2)
```

This results in

```
</html><h2>This is a second-level header</h2>
```

For the two methods just shown, there are convenience methods too: insert_before, insert_after.

The append method appends the new tag at the end of the tag. This means it behaves like the insert_after method.

```
soup.append(soup.new_tag('p'))
```

49

The preceding code results in the following:

```
</html><p></p>
```

The only difference is that the `insert_after` method is not implemented on soup objects, just on tags.

Anyway, with these methods you must pay attention where you insert or append new tags into the document.

Adding attributes to the tags is easy. Because tags behave like dictionaries, you can add new attributes the way you add keys and values to dictionaries.

```
soup.head['style'] = 'bold'
```

Even though the preceding code doesn't affect the rendered output, it added the new attribute to the head tag.

```
<head style="bold">
```

Changing Tags and Attributes

Sometimes you don't want to add new tags but want to change existing content. For example, you want to change the contents of paragraphs to be bold.

```
for p in soup.find_all('p', text=True):
    p.string.wrap(soup.new_tag('b'))
```

If you would like to change the contents of a tag that contains some formatting (like bold or italic tags), but you want to retain the contents, you can use the unwrap function.

```
soup = BeautifulSoup('<p> This is a <b>new</b> paragraph!</p>')
p = soup.p.b.unwrap()
print(soup.p)
```

Another example would be to change the id or the class of a tag. This works the same way as with adding new attributes: you can get the tag from the soup, and change the dictionary values.

```
for t in soup.findAll(True, id=True):
    t['class'] = 'withid'
    print(t)
```

The preceding example changes (or adds) the class withid to all tags that have an id attribute.

Deleting Tags and Attributes

If you want to delete a tag, you can use either extract() or decompose() on the tag.

extract() removes the tag from the tree and returns it, so you can use it in the future or add it to the HTML content at a different position.

decompose() deletes the selected tag permanently. No return values, no later usage; it is gone forever.

```
print(soup.title.extract())
print(soup.head)
```

Running the preceding code example with the example HTML of this section results in the following lines:

```
<title>Your Title Here</title>
<head>

</head>
```

Alternatively, you can change extract() to decompose().

```
print(soup.title.decompose())
print(soup.head)
```

Here, the result changes only in the first line where you don't get back anything.

```
None
<head>

</head>
```

Deletion doesn't only work for tags; you can remove attributes of tags too.

Imagine, you have tags that have an attribute called display, and you want to remove this display attribute from each tag. You can do it the following way:

```
for tag in soup.find_all(True, display=True):
    del tag['display']
```

If you now count the occurrences of tags having a display attribute, you will get 0.

```
print(len(soup.find_all(True, display=True)))
```

Finding Comments

Sometimes you need to find comments in HTML code to reverse-engineer JavaScript calls, because sometimes the content of a website is delivered in a comment and JavaScript renders it properly.

```
for comment in soup.find_all(text=lambda text:isinstance
(text, Comment)):
    print(comment)
```

The preceding code finds and prints **contents** of all comments. To make it work, you need to import Comments from the bs4 package too.

Converting a Soup to HTML Text

This is one of the easiest parts for Beautiful Soup because as you may know from your Python studies, everything is an object in Python, and objects have a method __str__ that returns the string representation of this object.

Instead of writing something like soup.__str__() every time, this method is called every time you convert the object to a string–for example when you print it to the console: print(soup).

However, this results in the same string representation as you provided in the HTML content. Moreover, you know, you can do better and provide a formatted string.

That's why Beautiful Soup has the prettify method. Per default, this method prints the pretty formatted version of the selected tag-tree. Yes, this means you can prettify your whole soup or just a selected subset of the HTML content.

```
print(soup.find('p').prettify())
```

This call results in (soup was created using the HTML from the beginning of this section)

```
<p>
 This is a new paragraph!
</p>
```

Extracting the Required Information

Now it is time to prepare your fingers and keyboard because you are about to create your first dedicated scraper, which will extract the required information, introduced in Chapter 2, from the Sainsbury's website.

All the source code shown in this chapter can be found in the file called bs_scraper.py in the source codes of this book.

However, I suggest, you start by trying to implement each functionality yourself with the tools and knowledge learned from this book already. I promise, it is not hard–and if your solution differs a bit from mine, don't worry. This is coding; every one of us has his/her style and approach. What matters is the result in the end.

Identifying, Extracting, and Calling the Target URLs

The first step in creating the scraper is to identify the links that lead us to product pages. In Chapter 2 we used Chrome's DevTools to find the corresponding links and their locations.

Those links are in an unordered list (`<ul>`), which has the class `categories departments`. You can extract them from the page with following code:

```
links = []
ul = soup.find('ul', class_='categories departments')
if ul:
    for li in ul.find_all('li'):
        a = li.find('a', href=True)
        if a:
            links.append(a['href'])
```

You now have the links that lead to pages listing products, each showing 36 at most.

However, some of these links lead to other groupings, which can lead to a third layer of grouping before you reach the product pages, just as you can see in Figure 3-1.

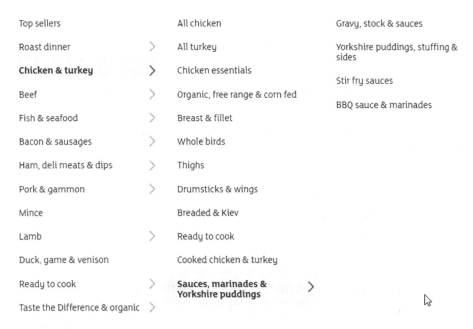

Top sellers	All chicken	Gravy, stock & sauces
Roast dinner >	All turkey	Yorkshire puddings, stuffing & sides
Chicken & turkey >	Chicken essentials	Stir fry sauces
Beef >	Organic, free range & corn fed	BBQ sauce & marinades
Fish & seafood >	Breast & fillet	
Bacon & sausages >	Whole birds	
Ham, deli meats & dips >	Thighs	
Pork & gammon >	Drumsticks & wings	
Mince	Breaded & Kiev	
Lamb >	Ready to cook	
Duck, game & venison	Cooked chicken & turkey	
Ready to cook >	**Sauces, marinades & Yorkshire puddings** >	
Taste the Difference & organic >		

Figure 3-1. *Three layers of navigation*

The navigation goes from "Chicken & turkey" to "Sauces, marinades & Yorkshire puddings," which leads to the third layer of links.

Therefore, your script should be able to navigate such chains too and get to the product listings.

```
product_pages = []
visited = set()
queue = deque()
queue.extend(department_links)
while queue:
    link = queue.popleft()
    if link in visited:
        continue
    visited.add(link)
    soup = get_page(link)
    ul = soup.find('ul', class_='productLister gridView')
```

```
if ul:
    product_pages.append(link)
else:
    ul = soup.find('ul', class_='categories shelf')
    if not ul:
        ul = soup.find('ul', class_='categories aisles')
    if not ul:
        continue
    for li in ul.find_all('li'):
        a = li.find('a', href=True)
        if a:
            queue.append(a['href'])
```

The preceding code uses the simple Breadth First Search (BFS) from the previous chapter to navigate through all the URLs until it finds the product lists. You can change the algorithm to Depth First Search(DFS); this results in a logically cleaner solution because if your code finds a URL that points to a navigation layer, it digs deeper until it finds all the pages.

The code looks first for shelves (`categories shelf`), which are the last layer of navigation prior to extracting `categories aisles`. This is because if it would extract aisles first and because all those URLs are already visited, the shelves and their content will be missing.

Navigating the Product Pages

In Chapter 2 you have seen that products can be listed on multiple pages. To gather information about every product, you need to navigate between these pages.

If you are lazy like me, you might come up with the idea to use the filter and set the product count to **108** per page, just like in Figure 3-2.

Figure 3-2. *Filter set to show 108 results*

Even though this is a good idea, it can happen that a category holds at least **109** products–and in this case, you need to navigate your script.

```
products = []
visited = set()
queue = deque()
queue.extend(product_pages)
while queue:
    product_page = queue.popleft()
    if product_page in visited:
        continue
    visited.add(product_page)
    soup = get_page(product_page)
    if soup:
        ul = soup.find('ul', class_='productLister gridView')
        if ul:
            for li in ul.find_all('li', class_='gridItem'):
                a = li.find('a', href=True)
                if a:
                    products.append(a['href'])
    next_page = soup.find('li', class_='next')
    if next_page:
        a = next_page.find('a', href=True)
        if a:
            queue.append(a['href'])
```

The preceding code block navigates through all the product lists and adds the URLs of the product sites to the list of products.

I used a BFS again, and a DFS would be OK too. The interesting thing is the handling of the next pages: you don't search for the numbering of the navigation but consecutively for the link pointing to the **next** page. This is useful for bigger sites, where you have umpteen-thousand pages. They won't be listed on the first site.[1]

Extracting the Information

You arrived at the product page. Now it is time to extract all the information required.

Because you already identified and noted the locations in Chapter 2, it will be a simple task to wire everything together.

Depending on your preferences, you can use dictionaries, named tuples, or classes to store information on a product. Here, you will create code using dictionaries and classes.

Using Dictionaries

The first solution you create will store the extracted information of products in dictionaries.

The keys in the dictionary will be the fields' names (which will be later used as a header in a CSV [Comma Separated Value], for example), the value the extracted information.

Because each product you extract has a URL, you can initialize the dictionary for a product as follows:

```
product = {'url': url}
```

I could list here how to extract all the information required, but I will only list the tricky parts. The other building blocks you should figure out yourself, as an exercise.

---

[1]Unless you are lucky. Once I encountered a site where all the links to the remaining pages were there in the HTML code but had been hidden with some JS-magic.

You can take a break, put down the book and try to implement the extractor. If you struggle with nutrition information or product origin, you will find help below.

If you are lazy, you can go ahead and find my whole solution later in this section or look at the source code provided for this book.

For me, the most interesting and lazy part is the extraction of the nutrition information table. It is a lazy solution because I used the table row headings as keys in the dictionary to store the values. They match the requirements, and therefore there is no need to add custom code that reads the table headers and decides which value to use.

```
table = soup.find('table', class_='nutritionTable')
    if table:
        rows = table.findAll('tr')
        for tr in rows[1:]:
            th = tr.find('th', class_='rowHeader')
            td = tr.find('td')
            if not th:
                product['Energy kcal'] = td.text
            else:
                product[th.text] = td.text
```

Extracting the product's origin was the most complicated part, at least in my eyes. Here you needed to find a header (<h3>) that contains a specific text and then its sibling. This sibling holds all the text but in a sheer format, which you need to make readable.

```
product_origin_header = soup.find('h3',
class_='productDataItemHeader', text='Country of Origin')
```

```
if product_origin_header:
    product_text = product_origin_header.find_next_sibling
    ('div', class_='productText')
    if product_text:
        origin_info = []
        for p in product_text.find_all('p'):
            origin_info.append(p.text.strip())
        product['Country of Origin'] = '; '.join
        (origin_info)
```

After implementing a solution, I hope you've got something similar to the following code:

```
Extracting product information into dictionaries
product_information = []
visited = set()
for url in product_urls:
    if url in visited:
        continue
    visited.add(url)
    product = {'url': url}
    soup = get_page(url)
    if not soup:
        continue  # something went wrong with the download
    h1 = soup.find('h1')
    if h1:
        product['name'] = h1.text.strip()

    pricing = soup.find('div', class_='pricing')
    if pricing:
        p = pricing.find('p', class_='pricePerUnit')
        unit = pricing.find('span', class_='pricePerUnitUnit')
        if p:
            product['price'] = p.text.strip()
```

```python
    if unit:
        product['unit'] = unit.text.strip()

label = soup.find('label', class_='numberOfReviews')
if label:
    img = label.find('img', alt=True)
    if img:
        product['rating'] = img['alt'].strip()
    reviews = reviews_pattern.findall(label.text.strip())
    if reviews:
        product['reviews'] = reviews[0]

item_code = soup.find('p', class_='itemCode')
if item_code:
    item_codes = item_code_pattern.findall(item_code.text.
    strip())
    if item_codes:
        product['itemCode'] = item_codes[0]

table = soup.find('table', class_='nutritionTable')
if table:
    rows = table.findAll('tr')
    for tr in rows[1:]:
        th = tr.find('th', class_='rowHeader')
        td = tr.find('td')
        if not th:
            product['Energy kcal'] = td.text
        else:
            product[th.text] = td.text

product_origin_header = soup.find('h3',
class_='productDataItemHeader', text='Country of Origin')
if product_origin_header:
    product_text = product_origin_header.find_next_
    sibling('div', class_='productText')
```

```
if product_text:
    origin_info = []
    for p in product_text.find_all('p'):
        origin_info.append(p.text.strip())
    product['Country of Origin'] = '; '.join(origin_info)
```

```
product_information.append(product)
```

As you can see in the preceding code, this is the biggest part of the scraper. But hey! You finished your very first scraper, which extracts meaningful information from a real website.

What you have probably noticed is the caution implemented in the code: every HTML tag is verified. If it does not exist, no processing happens; it would be a disaster and the application would crash.

The regular expressions to extract item codes and review counts is again a lazy way. Even though I am not a regex guru, I can create some simple patterns and use them for my purposes.

```
reviews_pattern = re.compile("Reviews \(((\d+)\)")
item_code_pattern = re.compile("Item code: (\d+)")
```

Using Classes

You can implement the class-based solution similarly to the dictionary-based one. The only difference is in the planning phase: while using a dictionary you don't have to plan much ahead, but with classes, you need to define the class model.

For my solution, I used a simple, pragmatic approach and created two classes: one holds the basic information; the second is a key-value pair for nutrition details.

I don't plan to go deep into OOP[2] concepts. If you want to learn more, you can refer to different Python books.

---

[2]OOP: object-oriented programming

As you already know, filling these objects is different too. There are different options for how to solve such a problem,[3] but I used a lazy version where I access and set every field directly.

Unforeseen Changes

While implementing the source code yourself, you may have found some problems and needed to react.

One of such changes could be the nutrition table. Even though we scrape one website, the rendering is not the same for all pages. Sometimes they display different elements or different styles. Moreover, sometimes the nutrition table contains different values than in the requirements, just like in Figures 3-3 and 3-4.

Table of Nutritional Information

	(cooked on the hob) per 100g	% adult RI per 100g	adult RI
Energy kJ	865	-	8400
Energy kcal	206	10%	2000
Fat	7.1g	10%	70g
of which			
- saturates	2.9g	15%	20g
- mono-unsaturates	3.9g	-	-
- polyunsaturates	0.3g	-	-
Carbohydrate	<0.5g	<1%	260g
of which sugars	<0.5g	<1%	90g
Fibre	<0.5g	-	-
Protein	35.5g	71%	50g
Salt	1.35g	23%	6g
RI = Reference Intakes of an average adult (8400kJ/2000kcal)			

Figure 3-3. *A different kind of nutrition table*

---

[3]For example, the Builder or Factory patterns, a constructor with all arguments.

Table of Nutritional Information

	per 100g	per slice	% adult RI per slice	adult RI
Energy kJ	505	141	-	8400
Energy kcal	120	33	2%	2000
Fat	2.4g	0.7g	1%	70g
of which				
- saturates	1.1g	0.3g	2%	20g
- mono-unsaturates	1.1g	0.3g	-	-
- polyunsaturates	<0.1g	<0.1g	-	-
Carbohydrate	<0.5g	<0.5g	<1%	260g
of which				
- sugars	<0.5g	<0.5g	<1%	90g
- starch	<0.5g	<0.5g	-	-
Fibre	<0.5g	<0.5g	-	-
Protein	24.4g	6.8g	14%	50g
Salt	1.00g	0.28g	5%	6g
RI = Reference Intakes of an average adult (8400J/2000kcal)				

Figure 3-4. *A third type of nutrition table*

What to do in such cases? Well, first, mention to your customer (if you have any) that you've found tables that contain nutrition information but in different details and format. Then think out a solution that is good for the outcome, and you don't have to create extra errands in your code to let it happen.

In my case, I went with the easiest solution and exported all I could from those tables. This means my results have fields that are not in the requirements and some can be missing, like *Total sugars*. Moreover, because the sublist of fats and carbohydrates has awkward dashes before each entry, or there are rows that contain only the text "of which," I adjusted the preceding code a bit to handle these cases.

```
table = soup.find('table', class_='nutritionTable')
if table:
    rows = table.findAll('tr')
    for tr in rows[1:]:
        th = tr.find('th', class_='rowHeader')
        td = tr.find('td')
        if not td:
            continue
        if not th:
            product['Energy kcal'] = td.text
        else:
            product[th.text.replace('-', ").strip()] = td.text
```

The exceptional case of *Energy* and *Energy kcal* (if not th) in the preceding code is fixed automatically in tables, which provide labels for every row.

Such changes are inevitable. Even though you get requirements and prepare your scraping process, exceptions in the pages can occur. Therefore, always be prepared and write code that can handle the unexpected, and you don't have to redo all the work. You can read more about how I deal with such thing later in this chapter.

Exporting the Data

Now that all information is gathered, we want to store it somewhere because keeping it in memory does not have much use for our customer.

In this section, you will see basic approaches to how you can save your information into a *CSV* or *JSON* file, or into a relational database, which will be SQLite.

Each subsection will create code for the following export objects: classes and dictionaries.

To CSV

A good old friend to store data is CSV. Python provides built-in functionality to export your information into this file type.

Because you implemented two solutions in the previous section, you will now create exports for both. But don't worry; you will keep both solutions simple.

The common part is the `csv` module of Python. It is integrated and has everything you need.

Quick Glance at the `csv` Module

Here you get a quick introduction into the `csv` module of the Python standard library. If you need more information or reference, you can read it online.[4]

I will focus on writing CSV files in this section; here I present the basics to give you a smooth landing on the examples where you write the exported information into CSV files.

For the code examples, I assume you did `import csv`.

Writing CSV files is easy: if you know how to write files, you are almost done. You must open a file-handle and create a CSV writer.

```
with open('result.csv', 'w') as outfile:
    spamwriter = csv.writer(outfile)⁵
```

The preceding code example is the simplest example I can come up with. However, there are a lot more options to configure, which sometimes will be important for you.

---

[4]`https://docs.python.org/3/library/csv.html`
[5]I have to admit, every time I write CSV files I use spamwriter as my variable's name. I guess this gives me a global understanding on what's happening.

- `dialect`: With the dialect parameter, you can specify formatting attributes grouped together to represent a common formatting. Such dialects are `excel` (the default dialect), `excel_tab`, or `unix_dialect`. You can define your own dialects too.

- `delimiter`: If you do/don't specify a dialect, you can customize the delimiter through this argument. This can be needed if you must use some special character for delimiting purposes because comma and escaping don't do the trick, or your specifications are restrictive.

- `quotechar`: As its name already mentions, you can override the default quoting. Sometimes your texts contain quote characters and escaping results in unwanted representations in MS Excel.

- `quoting`: Quoting occurs automatically if the writer encounters the delimiter inside a field's value. You can override the default behavior, and you can completely disable quoting (although I don't encourage you to do this).

- `lineterminator`: This setting enables you to change the character at the line's ending. It defaults to `'\r\n'` but in Windows you don't want this, just `'\n'`.

Most of the time, you are good to go without changing any of these settings (and relying on the Excel configuration). However, I encourage you to take some time and try out different settings. If something is wrong with your dataset and the export configuration, you'll get an exception from the csv module–and this is bad if your script already scraped all the information and dies at the export.

Line Endings

If you're working in a Windows environment like I do most of the time, it is a recommended practice to set the line ending for your writer. If not, you will get unwanted results.

```
with open('result.csv', 'w') as outfile:
    spamwriter = csv.writer(outfile)
    spamwriter.writerow([1,2,3,4,5])
    spamwriter.writerow([6,7,8,9,10])
```

The preceding code results in the CSV file in Figure 3-5.

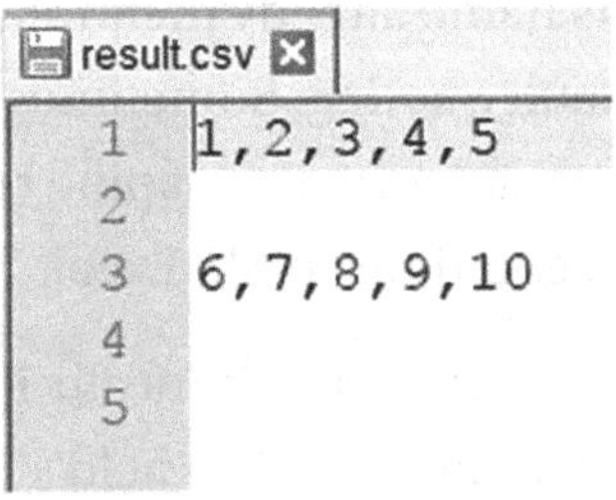

Figure 3-5. *The CSV file with too many empty lines*

To fix this, set the lineterminator argument to the writer's creation.

```
with open('result.csv', 'w') as outfile:
    spamwriter = csv.writer(outfile, lineterminator='\n')
    spamwriter.writerow([1,2,3,4,5])
    spamwriter.writerow([6,7,8,9,10])
```

Headers

What are CSV files without a header? Useful for those who know what to expect in which order, but if the order or number of columns changes, you can expect nothing good.

Writing the header works the same as writing a row: you must do it manually.

```
with open('result.csv', 'w') as outfile:
    spamwriter = csv.writer(outfile, lineterminator='\n')
    spamwriter.writerow(['average', 'mean', 'median', 'max',
    'sum'])
    spamwriter.writerow([1,2,3,4,5])
    spamwriter.writerow([6,7,8,9,10])
```

This results in the CSV file of Figure 3-6.

```
result.csv ☒
1   average,mean,median,max,sum
2   1,2,3,4,5
3   6,7,8,9,10
4
```

Figure 3-6. *CSV file with header*

Saving a Dictionary

To save a dictionary, Python has a custom writer object that handles this key-value pair object: the `DictWriter`.

This writer object handles mapping of dictionary elements to lines properly, using the keys to write the values into the right columns. Because of this, you must provide an extra element to the constructor of `DictWriter`: the list of field names. This list determines the order of the columns; and Python raises an error if a key is missing from the dictionary you want to write.

If the order of the result doesn't matter, you can easily set the field names when writing the results to the keys of the dictionary you want to write. However, this can lead to various problems: the order is not defined; it is mostly random on every machine you run it on (sometimes on the same machine too); and if the dictionary you choose is missing some keys, then your whole export is missing those values.

How to overcome this obstacle? For a dynamic solution, you can calculate the union[6] of all keys over all the resulted dictionaries. This ensures you won't encounter errors like the following:

```
ValueError: dict contains fields not in fieldnames:
'Monounsaturates', 'Sugars'
```

Alternatively, you can define the set of headers to use beforehand. In this case, you have power over the order of the fields, but you must know all the fields possible. This is not easy if you deal with dynamic key-value pairs just like the nutrition tables.

As you see, for both options you must create the list (set) of possible headers before you write your CSV file. You can do this by iterating through all product information and put the keys of each into a set, or you can add the keys in the extraction method to a global set.

Exporting to a CSV file looks like this.

```
with open('sainsbury.csv', 'w') as outfile:
    spamwriter = csv.DictWriter(outfile, fieldnames=get_field_
    names(product_information), lineterminator='\n')
    spamwriter.writeheader()
    spamwriter.writerows(product_information)
```

I hope your code is like this one. As you can see, I used an extra method to gather all the header-fields. However, as mentioned earlier, use the version that fits you better. My solution is slower because I iterate multiple times over the rows.

Saving a Class

The problem with using a class when working with a data-set like we get as we scrape Sainsbury's products is that we have no idea how the item will look in the end. That's because the nutrition tables can vary between two

---

[6]Set theory: `https://en.wikipedia.org/wiki/Union_(set_theory)`

products. To overcome this obstacle, you could write a key-normalization function that tries to map different keys of the product to one, and you can use this to map to the right property of your class. But this is a hard task and it won't fit into the scope of this book. Therefore, we will stick with the basic information we defined in the previous chapter and create a class based on that information.

```python
class Product:
    def __init__(self, url):
        self.url = url
        self.name = None
        self.item_code = None
        self.product_origin = None
        self.price_per_unit = None
        self.unit = None
        self.reviews = None
        self.rating = None
        self.energy_kcal = None
        self.energy_kj = None
        self.fat = None
        self.saturates = None
        self.carbohydrates = None
        self.total_sugars = None
        self.starc = None
        self.fibre = None
        self.protein = None
        self.salt = None
```

Even with this structure, you will need a minimal key-mapping from the table to the properties of the Product class. This is because there are some properties that need to be filled with values from the table that have a different name, for example total_sugars will get the value from the field *Total Sugars*.

Now with the class ready, let's modify the scraper to use Products instead of a dictionary. To save some space, I will only include the first few lines of the changed function.

```
def extract_product_information(product_urls):
    product_information = []
    visited = set()
    for url in product_urls:
        if url in visited:
            continue
        visited.add(url)
        product = Product(url)
        soup = get_page(url)
        if not soup:
            continue
        h1 = soup.find('h1')
        if h1:
            product.name = h1.text.strip()
```

As you can see, the code didn't change much; I highlighted the parts that are different. And you must modify your code in a similar fashion to fill the class' fields.

Now it is time to save the class to CSV. Without much fuss, here is my solution.

```
def write_results_to_csv(filename, rows):
    with open(filename, 'w') as outfile:
        spamwriter = csv.DictWriter(outfile, fieldnames=get_
        field_names(rows), lineterminator='\n')
        spamwriter.writeheader()
        spamwriter.writerows(map(lambda p: p.__dict__, rows))
```

And here is the get_field_names function.

```
def get_field_names(product_information):
    return set(vars(product_information[0]).keys())
```

Using the get_field_names method seems like a bit of overwork. If you feel like it, you can add the function's body instead of the method call, or create a method in the Product class that returns you the field names.

Again, this approach results in a nonpredictable order of columns in your CSV file. To ensure the order between runs and computers, you should define a fixed list for the fieldnames and use it for the export.

Another interesting code part is using the __dict__ method of the Product class. This is a handy built-in method to convert the properties of an instance object to a dictionary. The vars built-in function works like the __dict__ function and returns the variables of the given instance object as a dictionary.

To JSON

An alternative and more popular way to hold data is as JSON files. Therefore, you will create code blocks to export both dictionaries and classes to JSON files.

Quick Glance at the json module

This will be a quick introduction too. The json module of the Python standard library is huge, and you can find more information online.[7]

As in the CSV section, I'll focus on writing JSON files because the application writes the product information into JSON files.

I assume you did import json for the examples in this section.

---

[7]https://docs.python.org/3/library/json.html

Writing a JSON object to a file is as easy as it is with CSV, if not easier. You can simply tell the `json` module to write its contents to the given file-handle.

```
with open('result.json', 'w') as outfile:
    json.dump([{'average':12, 'median': 11}, {'average': 10,
    'median': 10}], outfile)
```

The preceding example writes the content (two dictionaries in a list) to the `result.json` file.

You can have some more control over the results. Because JSON objects in Python are most often dictionaries, you cannot guarantee the order of the keys in which they appear in the exported file. If you care about this (to have a consistent representation between runs), then you can set the `sort_keys` argument of the dump method to `True`. This will sort the dictionaries by their keys before writing them to the output.

```
with open('result.json', 'w') as outfile:
    json.dump([{'average':12, 'median': 11}, {'average': 10,
    'median': 10}],outfile, sort_keys=True)
```

Moreover, this is everything you need to know for now about writing data to JSON files.

Saving a Dictionary

As you have read in the previous section, writing results to JSON is easy, even easier than with CSV. Not just because JSON files are dictionaries (or lists of dictionaries), but also you don't have to care about the keys in the dictionary: if something is missing it won't bother the export. Sure, if you try to import the file's contents, then you must check if the current JSON object has the key you want to extract.

```
with open('sainsbury.json', 'w') as outfile:
    json.dump(product_information, outfile)
```

The preceding code saves the list filled with product information into the designated JSON file.

Saving a Class

Saving a class to a JSON file is not a trivial task, because classes are not your typical object to save into a JSON file.

Let's jump right into the code and write the method for exporting the results to a JSON file like the dictionary solution.

```
def write_results_to_json(filename, rows):
    with open(filename, 'w') as outfile:
        json.dump(rows, outfile)
```

Now if you run the scraper and arrive at the export method call, you will get an error like this one.

```
TypeError: Object of type 'Product' is not JSON serializable
```

The message tells you everything: an instance of the Product class is not serializable. To overcome this little obstacle, let's use our trick learned while exporting Product instances to a CSV file.

```
def write_results_to_json(filename, products):
    with open(filename, 'w') as outfile:
        json.dump(map(lambda p: p.__dict__, products), outfile)
```

This is not the final solution because a map isn't serializable either; we have to wrap it to an iterable.

```
def write_results_to_json(filename, rows):
    with open(filename, 'w') as outfile:
        json.dump(list(map(lambda p: p.__dict__, rows)),
            outfile)
```

To a Relational Database

Now you will learn how to connect to a database and write data into it. For the sake of simplicity, all the code will use SQLite because it doesn't require any installation or configuration.

The code you will write in this section will be database agnostic; you can port your code to populate any relational database (MySQL, Postgres).

The data you extracted in this chapter (and you will see throughout this book) doesn't need a relational database because it has no relations defined. I won't go into deeper detail on relational databases because my purpose is to get you going on your way to scraping, and many clients need their data in a MySQL table. Therefore, in this section, you will see how you can save the extracted information into an SQLite 3 database. The approach is similar to other databases. The only difference is that those databases need more configuration (like username, password, connection information), but there are plenty of resources available.

The first step is to decide on a database schema. One option is to put everything in a single table. In this case, you will have some empty columns, but you don't have to deal with dynamic names from the nutrition table. The other approach is to store common information (everything but the nutrition table) in one table and reference a second table with the key-value pairs.

The first approach is good when using dictionaries in the way this chapter uses them, because there you have all entries in **one** dictionary and it is hard to split the nutrition table from the other content. The second approach is good for classes, because there you already have two classes storing common information and the dynamic nutrition table.

Sure, there is a third approach: set the columns in stone and then you can skip the not needed/unknown keys, which result from different nutrition tables across the site. With this, you must take care of error handling and missing keys–but this keeps the schema maintainable.

To keep the example simple, I'm going with this third approach. The expected fields are defined in Chapter 2, and you can create a schema based on this list.

```
CREATE TABLE IF NOT EXISTS sainsburys (
    item_code INTEGER PRIMARY KEY,
    name TEXT NOT NULL,
    url TEXT NOT NULL,
    energy_kcal TEXT,
    energy_kjoule TEXT,
    fat TEXT,
    saturates TEXT,
    carbohydrates TEXT,
    total_sugars TEXT,
    starch TEXT,
    fibre TEXT,
    protein TEXT,
    salt TEXT,
    country_of_origin TEXT,
    price_per_unit TEXT,
    unit TEXT,
    number_of_reviews INTEGER,
    average_rating REAL
)
```

This DDL is SQLite 3; you may need to change it according to what database you're using. As you can see, we create the table only if it does not exist. This avoids errors and error handling when running the application multiple times. The primary key of the table is the product code. URL and product name cannot be null; for the other attributes you can allow null.

The interesting code comes when you add entries to the database. There can be two cases: you *insert* a new value, or the product is already in the table and you want to *update* it.

When you *insert* a new value, you must make sure the information contains every column by name, and if not, you must avoid exceptions. For the products of this chapter you could create a mapper that maps keys to their database representation prior to saving. I won't do this, but you are free to extend the examples as you wish.

When *updating*, there is already an entry in the database. Therefore, you must find the entry and update the relevant (or all) fields. Naturally, if you work with a historical dataset, then you don't need any updates, just inserts.

With SQLite, you can have both solutions in one query.

```
INSERT OR REPLACE INTO sainsburys
    values (?, ?, ?, ?, ?, ?, ?, ?, ?, ?, ?, ?, ?, ?, ?, ?, ?, ?)
```

Insert or replace solves the problem of identifying already existing entries in the database and updating them separately. Naturally, this solution works only for items where you have a fixed ID derived from the information to store in the database. If you use dynamically created technical IDs, then you need to figure out a way to find the corresponding entry in the database and update it, unless you want historical data stored in your database.

```
def save_to_sqlite(database_path, rows):
    global connection
    connection = __connect(database_path)
    __ensure_table()
    for row in rows:
        __save_row(row)
    __close_connection()

def __connect(database):
    return sqlite3.connect(database)
```

```python
def __close_connection():
    if connection:
        connection.close()

def __ensure_table():
    connection.execute(table_ddl)

def __save_row(row):
    connection.execute(sqlite_insert, (
        row.get('item_code'), row.get('name'), row.get('url'),
        row.get('Energy kcal'), row.get('Energy'),
        row.get('Fat'), row.get('Saturates'), row.
        get('Carbohydrates'), row.get('Total Sugars'),
        row.get('Starch'),
        row.get('Fibre'), row.get('Protein'), row.get('Salt'),
        row.get('Country of Origin'), row.get('price'),
        row.get('unit'), row.get('reviews'),
        row.get('rating')))
```

The preceding code is a sample example to save the entries in the database.

The main entry point is the save_to_sqlite function. The database_path variable holds the path to the target SQLite database. If it doesn't exist, the code will create it for you. The rows variable contains the data-dictionaries in a list.

The interesting part is the __save_row function. It saves a row, and as you can see, it requires a lot of information on the object you want to save. I use the get method of the dict class to avoid Key Errors if the given key is not present in the row to persist.

If you are using classes, I suggest you look at peewee,[8] an ORM[9] tool that helps you map objects to the relational database schema. It has built-in support for MySQL, PostgreSQL, and SQLite. In the examples, I will use peewee too because I like the tool.[10]

Here you can find a quick primer to peewee, where we will save data gathered into classes to the same SQLite database schema as previously.

To get started, you have to adapt the `Product` class; it has to extend the `peewee.Model` class, and the fields have to be peewee field types.

```python
from peewee import Model, TextField, IntegerField, DecimalField

class ProductOrm(Model):
    url = TextField()
    name = TextField()
    item_code = IntegerField
    product_origin = TextField()
    price_per_unit = TextField()
    unit = TextField()
    reviews = IntegerField()
    rating = DecimalField
    energy_kcal = TextField()
    energy_kj = TextField()
    fat = TextField()
    saturates = TextField()
    carbohydrates = TextField()
    total_sugars = TextField()
    starch = TextField()
    fibre = TextField()
    protein = TextField()
    salt = TextField()
```

---

[8]https://github.com/coleifer/peewee

[9]Object-relational mapping

[10]I have worked since 2007 with ORM tools, and I like the idea, but some queries can become quite complex.

This structure enables you to use the class later with **peewee** and store the information using ORM without any conversion. I named the class `ProductOrm` to show the difference from the previously used `Product` class.

To save an instance of the class, you simply must adapt the functions of the previous section.

We still must ensure that the database connection is open, and the target table exists. To do this, we utilize the functions we know, and which peewee has to offer.

```python
import peewee
from product import ProductOrm

def save_to_sqlite(database_path, rows):
    """
    This function saves all entries into the database
    :param database_path: the path to the SQLite file. If not
    exists, it will be created.
    :param rows: the list of ProductOrm objects elements to
    save to the database
    """

    __connect(database_path)
    __ensure_table()
    for row in rows:
        row.save()

def __connect(database):
    ProductOrm._meta.database = peewee.SqliteDatabase(database)

def __ensure_table():
    ProductOrm.create_table(True)
```

Here you can see that using peewee offers a slick version of saving. The database connection must be provided to the `Model` we use, and to adapt it dynamically, you have to access a protected field while you connect to the database. Alternatively, if you don't want to provide the target database dynamically, you could define it in the `ProductOrm` class too.

```python
import peewee

class ProductOrm(Model):
    url = TextField()
    name = TextField()
    item_code = IntegerField
    product_origin = TextField()
    price_per_unit = TextField()
    unit = TextField()
    reviews = IntegerField()
    rating = DecimalField
    energy_kcal = TextField()
    energy_kj = TextField()
    fat = TextField()
    saturates = TextField()
    carbohydrates = TextField()
    total_sugars = TextField()
    starch = TextField()
    fibre = TextField()
    protein = TextField()
    salt = TextField()

    class Meta:
        database = peewee.SqliteDatabase('sainsburys.db')
```

Any way you proceed, you can use peewee to take over all the action of persisting the data: creating the table and saving the data.

To create the table, you must call the `create_table` method on the `ProductOrm` class. With the `True` parameter provided, this method call will ensure that your target database has the table and if the table isn't there, it will be created. How will the table be created? This is based on the ORM model provided by you, the developer. `peewee` creates the DDL information based on the `ProductOrm` class: text fields will be `TEXT` database columns, and `IntegerField` fields will generate an `INTEGER` column.

And to save the entity itself, you must call the `save` method on the instantiated object itself. This removes all knowledge from you about the name of the target table, which parameters to save in which column, how to construct the `INSERT` statement... And this is just great if you ask me.

To an NoSQL Database

It would be a shame to forget about modern databases, which are state of the art. Therefore, in this section, you will export the gathered information into a MongoDB.

If you are familiar with this database and followed along with my examples in this book, you already know how I will approach the solution: I will use previous building blocks. In this case, the JSON export.

An NoSQL database is a good fit because most of the time they are designed to store documents that share few or no relations with other entries in the database–at least they shouldn't do it excessively.

Installing MongoDB

Unlike SQLite, you must install MongoDB on your computer to get it running.

In this section, I won't go into detailed instructions on how to install and configure MongoDB; it is up to you, and their homepage has very good documentation,[11] especially for Python developers.

I assume for this section you installed MongoDB and the Python library: `PyMongo`. Without this, it will be hard for you to follow the code examples.

---

[11]https://docs.mongodb.com/getting-started/python/

Writing to MongoDB

As previously, I will focus only on writing to the target database because the scraper stores information but won't read any entries from the database.

Writing to an NoSQL database like MongoDB is easier because it doesn't require a real structure and you can put everything into it as you wish. Sure, it would be ridiculous to do such things; we need structure to avoid chaos. However, theoretically, you can just jam everything into your database.

Saving the "basic" dictionary to the MongoDB database works straight out of the box. Because the database stores objects as they are, you don't have to do any conversions. And you can reuse the code for saving to a JSON file. Yes, even for classes.

```python
import pymongo

connection = None
db = None

def save_to_database(database_name, products):
    global connection
    __connect(database_name)
    for product in products:
        __save(product)
    __close_connection()

def __save(product):
    db['sainsburys'].insert_one(product.__dict__)

def __connect(database):
    global connection, db
    connection = pymongo.MongoClient()
    db = connection[database]
```

```
def __close_connection():
    if connection:
        connection.close()
```

My version is like the SQL-version. I open the connection to the provided database and insert each product into the MongoDB database. To get the JSON representation of the product, I use the __dict__ variable.

If you want to insert a collection into the database, use insert_many instead of insert_one.

If you are interested in using a library like peewee just for MongoDB and ODM (Object-Document Mapping), you can take a look at MongoEngine.

Performance Improvements

If you put the code of this chapter together and run the extractor, you will see how slow it is.

Serial operations are always slow, and depending on your network connection, it can be slower than slow. The parser behind Beautiful Soup is another point where you can gain some performance improvements, but this is not a big boost. Moreover, what happens if you encounter an error right before finishing the application? Will you lose all data?

In this section, I'll try to give you options for how you can handle such cases, but it is up to you to implement them.

You could create benchmarks of the different solutions in this section, but as I mentioned earlier in this book, it makes no sense because the environment always changes, and you cannot ensure that your scripts run in exactly the same conditions.

Changing the Parser

One way to improve Beautiful Soup is to change the parser that it uses to create the object model out of the HTML content.

Beautiful Soup can use the following parsers:

- html.parser

- lxml (install with pip install lxml)

- html5lib (install with pip install html5lib)

The default parser, which is already installed with the Python standard library, is html.parser–as you have already seen in this book.

Changing the parser doesn't give such a speed boost that you will see the difference right away, just some minor improvements. However, to see some flawed benchmarking, I added a timer that starts at the beginning of the script and prints the time needed to extract all the 3,005 products without writing them to any storage.

Table 3-1 shows a comparison between the different parsers available with Beautiful Soup while scraping the 3,005 products of the "Meat & fish" department.

Table 3-1. *Some Execution Speed Comparisons*

Parser	Entries	Time taken (in seconds)
html.parser	3,005	2,347.9281
lxml	3,005	2167.9156
lxml-xml	3,005	2457.7533
html5lib	3,005	2,544.8480

As you can see, the difference is significant. lxml wins the game because it is a well-defined parser written in C, and therefore it can work extremely fast on well-structured documents.

html5lib is very slow; its only advantage is that it creates valid HTML5 code from any input.

Choosing a parser has trade-offs. If you need speed, I suggest you install lxml. If you cannot rely on installing any external modules to Python, then you should go with the built-in html.parser.

Any way you decide, you must remember: if you change the parser, the parse tree of the soup changes. This means you must revisit and perhaps change your code.

Parse Only What's Needed

Even with an optimized parser, creating the document model of the HTML text takes time. The bigger the page, the more slowly this model is created.

One option to tune the performance a bit is to tell Beautiful Soup which part of the whole page you will need, and it will create the object model from the relevant part. To do this, you can use a SoupStrainer object.

A SoupStrainer tells Beautiful Soup what parts extract, and the parse tree will consist only of these elements. This speeds up the process a bit, if you can narrow down the required information to a smaller portion of the HTML.

```
strainer = SoupStrainer(name='ul', attrs={'class':
'productLister gridView'})
soup = BeautifulSoup(content, 'html.parser', parse_
only=strainer)
```

The preceding code creates a simple SoupStrainer that limits the parse tree to unordered lists having a class attribute 'productLister gridView'–which helps to reduce the site to the required parts–and it uses this strainer to create the soup.

Because you already have a working scraper, you can replace the soup calls using a strainer to speed up things.

The following piece of information is hard to find on the Internet: you can use multiple attributes in the strainer to parse the website. For example, if you extract the links to product pages, you have three options based on the level of the current department link:

- The link leads to product pages.

- The link leads to a first-level sublist.

- The link leads from a first-level sublist to a second-level sublist.

In this case, you have three different classes but want to create the soup if any of them is present. You can do something like this:

```
BeautifulSoup(content, 'html.parser', name='ul',
              attrs={'class': ['productLister gridView',
              'categories shelf', 'categories aisles']})
```

Here, you have listed all three versions of the lists that can happen, and the soup contains all the relevant information.

A (flawed) benchmark using a hard cache:[12] my script gained 100% speedup (from 158.907 seconds to 79.109 seconds) using strainers.

Saving While Working

If your application encounters an exception while running, the current version breaks on the spot and all your gathered information is lost.

One approach is to use DFS. With this approach, you go straight down the target graph and extract the products in the shortest way. Moreover,

---

[12]Hard cache: Get all information from the cache, and if there are attempts to gather anything from the Internet, refuse it. This makes scraping a bit consistent between runs.

when you encounter a product, you save it to your target medium (CSV, JSON, relational, or NoSQL database).

Another approach keeps the BFS and applies saving the products as they are extracted. This is the same approach as using the DFS algorithm. The only difference is when you reach the products.

Both approaches need a mechanism to restart work, or at least save some time with skipping already written products. For this, you create a function that loads the contents of the target file, stores the extracted URLs in memory, and skips the download of already extracted products.

Staying with the BFS solution of this chapter, you must modify the `extract_product_information` function to `yield` every piece of product information when it is ready. Then you wrap the call of this method into a loop and save the results to your target.

Surely, this creates some overhead: you open a file-handle every time you save a piece, you must take care of saving the entries into a JSON array, you open and close database connections for every write... Alternatively, you do opening and closing (file-handle or database connection) surrounding the extraction. In those cases, you must take care of flushing/committing the results; if something happens, your extracted data is saved.

What about try-except?   Well, wrapping the whole extracting code in a `try-except` block is a solution too, but you must ensure that you don't forget about the exceptions that happened and you can get the missing data later. But such exceptions can happen while you're at a main page that leads to detail pages—and from my experience I know that once you wrap code into an exception handling block, you will forget to revisit the issues in the future.

Developing on a Long Run

Sometimes you develop scrapers for bigger projects, and you cannot launch your script after every change because it takes too much time.

Even though this scraper you implemented is short and extracts around 3,000 products, it takes some time to finish—and if you have an error in the data extraction, it is always time-consuming to fix the error and start over.

In such cases I utilize caching of results of intermediate steps; sometimes I cache the HTML codes themselves. This section is about my approach and my opinions.

Because you already have deep Python knowledge, this section is again an optional read: feel free if you know how to utilize such approaches.

Caching Intermediate Step Results

The first thing I always did when I started working with a basic, self-written spider just like the one in this example was to cache intermediate step results.

Applying this approach to this chapter's code, you export the resulting URLs after each step into a file and change the application so that it reads the file of the last step back when it starts and skips the scraping until the following step.

Your challenge in such cases is to write your code to continue work where it went down. With intermediate results, this can mean you have to scrape the biggest part of the websites again because your script died before it could save all information on products—or it died while it was about to save the extracted information.

This step is not bad, because you have a checkpoint where you can continue if you step messes up. But honestly, this requires much extra work, like saving the intermediate steps **and** loading them back for each stage. And because I am lazy and learned a lot while on my development journey, I use the next solution as the basis for all my scraping tasks.

Caching Whole Websites

A better approach is to cache whole websites locally. This gives better performance in the long run for rerunning your script every time.

When implementing this approach, I extend the functionality of the website gathering method to route over a cache: if the requested URL is in the cache, return the cached version; if it's not present, gather the site and store the result in the cache.

You can use file-based or database caches to store the websites while you're developing. In this section you will learn both approaches.

The basic idea for the cache is to create a key that identifies the website. Keys are unique identifiers, and a web page's URL is unique too. Therefore, let's use this as the key, and the content of the page is the value.

But we have some limitations (Table 3-2): these URLs can get very long, and some solutions have limitations on the keys, like length or contained characters.

Table 3-2. *Limitations by Operating Systems*

Operating system	File system	Invalid filename characters	Maximum filename length
Linux	Ext3/Ext4	/ and \0	255 bytes
OS X	HFS Plus	: and \0	255 UTF-16 code units
Windows	NTFS	\, /, ?, :, *, ", >, <, and |	255 characters

Therefore, I suggest a simple solution: create a hash based on the URL.

Hashes are short and if you choose a good algorithm, you can avoid collision for a large number of pages. I'll use the `hashlib.blake2b` hash function because it is faster than the commonly used hashes (MD5 for example) and it's as secure as SHA-3[13]. Also, this algorithm generates 128 characters, which is short enough for all three dominating operating systems.

---

[13]For more information, visit: `https://blake2.net/`

File-Based Cache

The first approach that comes into the mind of old-school developers (like me) is to save pages to files. This is the easiest solution because to write files you don't need a database, you only write permissions. And most of the time this is present because you develop your scrapers locally. For the production run there is no need to cache the website if you run once. If you do multiple runs, then you must deal with cache invalidation (look at a later section).

The only things you must implement are three functions: initializing the cache, retrieving the requested URL's content from the cache, and saving a URLs content to the filesystem. Because the functionality can be well encapsulated, I decided to implement my cache as a class. You don't need to follow my approach; use a programming style that best fits your needs and skills (likes).[14]

Database Cache

An alternative solution is to save the websites into a database. There are again two options: using a relational database or an NoSQL one. Because websites are documents, I suggest you try using an NoSQL database. But for completeness, I'll show you both approaches in this section.

As for the product details, in this section I'll use SQLite 3 as the relational database. The cache is as simple as the file cache: the class must load the cache from the database and save new content to the database. The only difference is that the system in the background is a database.

My approach was the same as with the file-based version: load the contents of the database into memory and use this cache to return the contents. That's because it makes the script much faster!

---

[14]Alternatively, to be more consistent, you can create a downloader, which hides the cache from the users of your code.

I don't want to create benchmarks here. You must decide for yourself how you can utilize your memory usage and disk reads. For many websites, keeping the content in memory is cheap.

I use the same ID generated from the URL because it's good enough and makes a good primary key too. Some people rely on technical IDs (autogenerated, numeric identifiers), but for this website the generated ID or simply using the URL fits well.

Saving Space

Saving the target website locally can occupy a lot of space. Saving the Sainsbury's website with this approach takes 253 MB of space. With current computers this is not a big thing, but this is only one web page–a small portion of the whole website. Perhaps you have multiple websites you scrape and with time the occupied space grows, and you want to save space. If you don't want to, then skip this section.

You can save space by compressing the contents of the page either while using files or a database. This requires only a modification in your saver and loader methods, and the usage of zlib. When saving, you should compress the contents, and when you're reading the file back, you should decompress it.

Because you're using Python 3 and zlib requires a bytes-like object to compress, you must encode and decode the strings.

To compare the difference, my file-based cache requires 253 MB of space; after I switched to compression, it required only 49 MB. What a difference!

But every rose has its thorn: saving space requires more computation time for decompressing the content. On my computer with the currently saved dataset, the scraper runs 31 seconds slower when decompressing. This may not sound bad, but proportionally this is 17% more time. But if you compare this result with the running times with different parsers, then you saved over 90% of your running time while working on the fine details of your script. And you don't overload the website because you run your script 100 times daily.

Updating the Cache

Another part to take into consideration while developing caches is the invalidation time. When an entry in a cache is invalid, when should the parser download it again?

There is no exact answer to this question. You should think about the website you're scraping and then set a value for the timeout.

For a web shop I'd use one week, but one day at least because the only thing that can change in a product is its price and its reviews. Other information will not change so often.

If you look at the example code and the target website of this chapter, you will come up with the idea to store only product pages in the cache. Why? If you store all the pages, you don't get information on new products added until the page containing the product details is discarded because of its age. But you won't navigate away from the product pages, so they are a good target to cache every time and refresh them once a week–if reviews don't matter as much.

The approach of caching is nothing complicated. For file-based caching you must look at the file's modification date, and if it is older than the grace period, you can remove it from the cache (and delete the file). For databases, you should add the modification timestamp to the entity you're saving. Then the protocol is the same: if the entry is too old, delete it and then the scraper does its job and downloads the site anew.

Source Code for this Chapter

You can find all the code created for this chapter as whole parsers in the chapter_03 folder of the sources.

- `basic_scraper.py` contains the basic scraper, which extracts the information into dictionaries. It doesn't have any performance tuning, but you can change the parser used by `Beautiful Soup` to gain some minor improvements.

- `basic_scraper_using_classes.py` contains an extended version of the basic scraper: it uses classes to store the extracted information and saves those classes to an SQLite and a MongoDB datasource.

- `file_cache.py` contains the file-based cache that stores the downloaded pages on your filesystem. The final solution uses compression with `zlib` and discards old entries on startup.

- `downloader.py` contains a downloader, which hides the cache and downloading process from your scraper. You can transparently switch caches and perhaps do some combination on the caches too to enable migration from one cache to another. Feel free to try things out!

Summary

In this chapter you learned a lot, such as how to use `Beautiful Soup` and `requests` together, and you created your first full scraper application, which gathers the requirements from Chapter 2.

The scraper exported the gathered results into different stores, like CSV, JSON, and databases.

But every rose has its thorn: you learned about bottlenecks of this simpler solution, and applied some techniques to make it perform better. And with this you've learned how complex it can be to write your own scraper.

And even with such a lengthy chapter, there are some points still untouched, for example, honoring the `robots.txt` file. You can extend the code from this chapter to honor the robots.txt file of the website; you have the building blocks to do so.

In the next chapter you will learn `Scrapy`, the website scraping tool for Python, which leverages these optimizations from your shoulders. The only things you must do are create the extractor code and configure `Scrapy` properly.

CHAPTER 4

Using Scrapy

After a lengthy introduction to Beautiful Soup and custom scrapers, it's time to look at Scrapy: **the** website scraping tool for Python.

In my opinion, this is the only viable tool available currently for Python, which can handle complex scraping tasks out of the box. You can cache web pages, and add parallelism as you wish; you only need to configure Scrapy properly and write the extraction code.

In this chapter you will learn how to get the most out of Scrapy for the majority of your website scraping projects. You will write the Sainsbury's extractor, configure Scrapy to create a website-friendly spider, and you will learn how to apply custom exporting options to the extracted information.

As opposed to the previous chapter, where I introduced Beautiful Soup at the beginning and you created the project to scrape the Sainsbury's website afterward, now you will learn the basics of Scrapy through implementing the project scraper. Toward the end of this chapter I'll add more information and insights into the tools that we didn't use for the project, but I think it is useful to know if you write your own scrapers in the future.

Ready? Why not!

© Gábor László Hajba 2018

G. L. Hajba, *Website Scraping with Python*, https://doi.org/10.1007/978-1-4842-3925-4_4

Installing **Scrapy**

Your first task is to install Scrapy to your Python environment.

To install Scrapy, simply execute

```
pip install scrapy
```

And that's it. With this command you installed all requirements too, so you're ready to create scraper projects.

Note   The developers of Scrapy recommend installing the tool into a virtual environment. This is a good practice to have a clean version of your scraping tool; and this hinders you from updating a dependency of Scrapy to a noncompatible version, which will render your scraper nonworking.

If you have a hard time installing Scrapy, just read their instructions.[1]

Creating the Project

To get started with Scrapy, you have to create a project. This helps you to keep order in your files and focus on only one problem. To create a new project, simply execute the following command:

```
scrapy startproject sainsburys
```

This call results in something like this:

```
New Scrapy project 'sainsburys', using template directory
'c:\\python\\scrapy\\lib\\site-packages\\scrapy\\templates\\
project', created in:
    C:\scraping_book\chapter_4\sainsburys
```

---

[1]https://docs.scrapy.org/en/latest/intro/install.html#intro-install

You can start your first spider with

```
cd sainsburys
scrapy genspider example example.com
```

Depending on the OS you use and the location where you have your projects, the preceding text can vary. However, what matters is the information about how you can create your first spider.

But before you create your first spider, let's look at the file structure created, as shown in Figure 4-1.

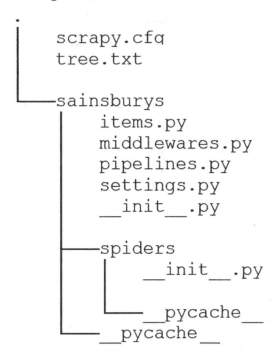

Figure 4-1. *The project structure*

The structure should be similar; if not, perhaps something changed in the new version of Scrapy you are using.

Configuring the Project

Before you dive into the code of the main scraper you will implement with Scrapy, you should configure your project properly. Basic configuration is required to show you are a "good citizen," and your spider is a well-raised tool too.

The basic configuration I suggest you do **every time** is to add the user agent and see that the robots.txt file is honored.

Fortunately, the basic project skeleton of Scrapy comes with a configuration file where most of the settings are set properly or are commented out but tell you about the option and which values it accepts. You can find the configuration of the project in the settings.py file.

If you take a look at it, you will see a lot of options added; most of them are commented out. The default values work perfectly fine for most scraping projects, but you can tune them if you think it gives you better performance or you need some more complexity added.

The two properties I always use are

- USER_AGENT

- ROBOTSTXT_OBEY

The names of these properties already tell you what they are good for.

For the USER_AGENT, you see a default that consists of the bot's name (sainsburys) and an example domain. I change it mostly to a Chrome agent. You can obtain one through the DevTools of Chrome: you open the *Network* tab, load a web page normally in your browser, click on the request in the *Network* tab, and copy the value of **User Agent** in the *Headers* tab of the request. This works even if you are offline.

And to be a good citizen, leave the ROBOTSTXT_OBEY on True. With this, Scrapy takes care of handling the contents of the robots.txt file if one is present.

I suggest you delete all commented-out settings. This will help you in reading the file later and you see all active configuration at once; you do not have to scroll through all the lines to see which is commented out. It is hard even in an IDE with good color coding.

Besides these properties, I suggest you add CONCURRENT_REQUESTS = 1. This reduces the speed of the spider, **but** while testing, you will run the code quite a lot and you don't want to get banned from the website right at the beginning–or you don't want the website's servers to be done just because you (and 99,999 other readers) run the scraper simultaneously and the servers cannot handle the load. If you look at the commented code, you'll find that the default value for this is 16. I'll add a section where I will turn up the number of parallel requests and will do a flawed microbenchmark.

To summarize: my final settings.py file looks like this:

```
# -*- coding: utf-8 -*-

BOT_NAME = 'sainsburys'

SPIDER_MODULES = ['sainsburys.spiders']
NEWSPIDER_MODULE = 'sainsburys.spiders'

USER_AGENT = 'Mozilla/5.0 (Windows NT 10.0; Win64; x64)
             AppleWebKit/537.36' \
             '(KHTML, like Gecko) Chrome/63.0.3239.84
             Safari/537.36'

ROBOTSTXT_OBEY = True

CONCURRENT_REQUESTS = 1
```

In the preceding code you can see an example of a Windows 10 Chrome user agent string. You don't have to stick with this: feel free to use the one from your browser; it won't make any difference.

Now that the basic configuration is done, we can implement the spider that will do the work for us.

Terminology

While setting the configuration, you have had the option to learn some of Scrapy's terminology, like **middleweare** or **pipeline**. They are the building blocks of this scraper, where you can implement your own code and extend the functionality if it is missing something you need.

Middleware

Middlewares are hooks into Scrapy; this means, you can extend the already available functionality. There are two types of middlewares in Scrapy:

- Downloader middlewares

- Spider middlewares

As their names already suggest, you can either extend the downloader (add your own cache, proxy the calls, modify requests prior sending, or ignore requests, just as a few examples), or the parser functionality (filter out some responses, handle spider exceptions, call different functions based on the response, etc.).

For basic scraping there's no need to write your own middlewares, because you can get along well with the tools available–and as Scrapy is evolving, more custom code gets into the standard library.

Middlewares need to be activated in the settings.py file.

```
DOWNLOADER_MIDDLEWARES = {
    'yourproject.middlewares.CustomDownloader': 500
}
```

```
SPIDER_MIDDLEWARES = {
    'yourproject.middlewares.SpiderMiddleware': 211
}
```

If you have your middlewares but they don't seem to work, you might have forgotten to activate them. Another reason could be that they are executed at the wrong position: the number you provide as the value in the dictionary tells Scrapy about the order in which the middleware should be executed:

- For downloader middlewares, the process_request method is called in *increasing* order.

- For downloader middlewares, the process_response method is called in *decreasing* order.

- For spider middlewares, the process_spider_input method is called in *increasing* order.

- For spider middlewares, the process_spider_output method is called in *decreasing* order.

Therefore, it can happen that you expect something in the request/response / input/output, but it was handled by a middleware with a lower/higher priority.

Pipeline

Pipelines handle the extracted data. This involves cleaning, formatting, and sometimes exporting the data. Even though Scrapy has built-in pipelines that export your data in a given format (CSV, JSON—more on these later in this chapter), sometimes you need to write your own pipeline to configure the result to meet your (your customers') expectations.

You will write more pipelines than middlewares while you're working as a pro scraper. Nevertheless, it is not as bad as it might sound. In this chapter we will create a simple item pipeline to show you how it is done.

Similar to middlewares, you have to activate your pipelines in the settings.py file.

```
ITEM_PIPELINES = {
    'yourproject.pipelines.MongoPipeline': 418
}
```

Extension

Extensions are singleton classes that get instantiated once at startup and contain custom code, which you can use to add some custom functionality that is not related to downloading or scraping like a middleware does. Such extensions can be used for logging, or monitoring memory consumption (these are already built-in extensions).

Extensions can be loaded the same way as middlewares and pipelines in settings.py.

```
EXTENSIONS = {
    'scrapy.extensions.memusage.CoreStats': 500
}
```

Selectors

This is the most important term you will encounter while using Scrapy. Selectors are the code parts that select certain parts of the HTML. As you can see, selectors work similar to Beautiful Soup and lxml but they are the Scrapy version, and you can use XPath or CSS expressions.

I prefer XPath expressions because I worked for years with XML and XML transformations; therefore, I know XPath expression well. You are free to use any approach, but I will stick to XPath.

Selectors are objects in Scrapy, and because of this they can be constructed from a text.

```
from scrapy.selector import Selector

selector = Selector(text='<html><body><h1>Hello Selectors!</h1>
</body></html>')
print(selector.xpath('//h1/text()').extract()) # ['Hello
Selectors!']
```

or from a response:

```
from scrapy.selector import Selector
from scrapy.http import HtmlResponse

response = HtmlResponse(url='http://my.domain.com',
body='<html><body><h1>Hello Selectors!</h1></body></html>',
encoding='UTF-8')
print(Selector(response=response).css('h1::text').extract()) #
['Hello Selectors!']
```

However, because selectors are the way to extract data, you can conveniently access them from your response using

```
response.xpath()
```

or

```
response.css()
```

And this makes Scrapy a great tool in my opinion: you don't have to bother creating selector objects, but use the available convenient method accesses.

Follow the links if you want to read more about CSS selectors[2] or XPath expressions.[3]

---

[2]www.w3.org/TR/selectors/
[3]www.w3.org/TR/xpath/all/

Implementing the Sainsbury Scraper

To start working on the extraction code, you will need a spider generated. As you have seen in the previous section, where you created and configured the base of the project, you can do it with the `genspider` command. Let's do it right now. First change the directory to the one where you generated your bot, and then execute the following command:

```
scrapy genspider sainsburys 'https://www.sainsburys.co.uk/shop/
gb/groceries/meat-fish/'
```

When executing the preceding command, you get a strange message:

```
Cannot create a spider with the same name as your project
```

Well, if we cannot get a spider with the same name, let's give it a different name. My suggestion is a name that is easy to remember for you. I use mostly `"basic"` because it's easy to write and I have a basic scraper to do the extraction for me. The project already has a unique name; and with basic I can always start my spiders, regardless of the project.

```
scrapy genspider basic https://www.sainsburys.co.uk/shop/gb/
groceries/meat-fish
```

The response now is different.

```
Created spider 'basic' using template 'basic' in module:
  sainsburys.spiders.basic
```

With this command, Scrapy added a `basic.py` file to the project's spiders folder. This file will be the base of your spider; here will you implement the extraction code.

The code looks normal, but if you look thoroughly, you will see that the `start_urls` variable looks a bit weird.

```
start_urls = ['http://https://www.sainsburys.co.uk/shop/gb/
groceries/meat-fish/']
```

It has an extra `http://`. This is because of the URL we provided for the scraper generation. `Scrapy` is meant to scrape a domain; therefore, you should provide a domain for the spider creation. However, in the particular case of the example, we will scrape only a subset of the whole domain ("Meat & fish"). There are two options:

- You create the spider using only the domain `'www.sainsburys.co.uk'` and add the remaining part of the URL later to the start_urls (or change the entry completely).

- you simply remove the extra `'http://'` from the start_urls entry.

What's This `allowed_domains` About?

If you looked at the code thoroughly, you have seen there's a list of allowed domains. This list is used to give the spider a bound. Without setting the allowed domains, you could write a script that goes through the Internet (following every link on the pages it scrapes). For most purposes, you want to keep your scraping in one domain. **However**, sometimes you have to deal with internal or subdomains. In those cases, you can extend this list manually to fix such "issues."

And here you should set the domain only. When you generated the spider, it added the whole URL to this list, but you need something like this:

```
allowed_domains = ['www.sainsburys.co.uk']
```

You can find the source code for an empty project with my default configuration among the sources for this chapter in the folder `01_empty_project`.

Preparation

This section is brief. If you followed along, you have everything configured and there is no need for any other preparation.

Just a quick checklist to see if you are ready to go:

- You've read the requirements of Chapter 2.

- You've created a Scrapy-project.

- You've configured the project as described in this chapter.

- You've created a spider.

If anything is missing, take the time to fix it; then you are good to follow along.

Using the Shell

One function of Scrapy I like to utilize for preparation work is to use its shell, which gives us an environment to test and prepare code snippets for extraction. And because the shell behaves just like your spider code will, it is ideal for creating the building blocks of your application.

With a naive approach (or similar, like we did in the previous chapter), you'd write a part of your code and run the spider. If there's an error, you'd fix the code and rerun the spider. This is OK if the website doesn't limit access based on requests. If there's a limit, you may end up exceeding it and your spider (and your computer, current IP, whole company network[4]) is banned from the website. And, as I have seen, Sainsbury's runs behind CloudFlare–you better not send parallel requests to their website!

---

[4]Once our client was banned from StackOverflow (SO) for too many requests in a minute. Around 100 software developers have had a hard time without SO.

The Scrapy shell works differently: it downloads your target web page and you can create your extraction logic on this copy. If you need to move to another page, you let the shell download it and you are good to write the next chunk of code.

Starting the shell is easy.

```
scrapy shell
```

You can pass along a <url> parameter, which is your target URL.

For this book we will use https://www.sainsburys.co.uk/shop/gb/groceries/meat-fish/:

```
scrapy shell https://www.sainsburys.co.uk/shop/gb/groceries/meat-fish/
```

Alternatively, you can also fetch the URL when you open Scrapy's shell without any, or with a different URL.

```
>>> fetch('https://www.sainsburys.co.uk/shop/gb/groceries/meat-fish/')
```

Now the shell has downloaded the web page behind the URL. This means two things: now you have access to the *Meat & Fish* page's content and can try your extractors; and second, you have to download every page you want to use in the shell. Even though the second point sounds bad, it is not: getting other pages is made easy in Scrapy and therefore in the shell too.

In the shell you have access to a response object (just like in the parse method, which we will write later in this chapter), and with this response you can use the available selectors.

I don't want to dig very deep into how to use the shell to prepare your scraper script. Therefore, we will do one example: we get the URLs to the next page. This will give you a good start and the feel of using the shell for further preparation.

As you may remember, the links that lead to the detailed pages can be found in an unordered list (`<ul class="categories departments">`). The list's elements (`<li>`) have an anchor child (`<a>`), and the value of the href attribute of these anchors is the URL we are looking for.

To get the list of these URLs, you can write the following code using XPath:

```
urls = response.xpath('//ul[@class="categories departments"]/
li/a/@href').extract()
```

Using CSS selectors, this would look like this:

```
urls = response.css('ul.categories.departments > li >
a::attr(href)').extract()
```

And that is it. You have all the URLs that lead to either product listings of the category or to a site containing more subcategories, just like in the previous chapter.

I suggest you dig a bit deeper into XPath and CSS selectors for now, to understand the extractor code that you will write starting with the next section.

def parse(self, response)

Now we are good to go to write the code in the `basic.py` file.

The `parse` method is the core of every spider. This method is called every time Scrapy downloads a URL, and most of the time you write your extraction code in this method.

The `response` argument holds the response from calling the URL. It can contain the website's content but sometimes you can get back error codes, for example, when the website is down or nonexistent.

You can write a whole scraper into the `parse` method, but I suggest organizing your code into methods (and actually, this is the suggested practice of many developers). This helps you in the future to understand what the code wants to achieve.

Therefore, the parse function will be very sparse: it extracts only the URLs to the category pages (the same from the preparation with the shell), and initiates the download and parsing of those pages.

```
from scrapy import Request

# some code left out...

def parse(self, response):
    urls = response.xpath('//ul[@class="categories
    departments"]/li/a/@href').extract()

    for url in urls:
        yield Request(url, callback=self.parse_department_
        pages)
```

The preceding code extracts the href attributes of every anchor element of the list of the desired class. The interesting part is how the scraping is continued: you yield a new Request object with the target URL as the first parameter and the callback function that should be called if the server returns an OK-ish response for the given URL. In this case it will be the parse_department_pages method of this same class.

There's an alternative way to get to the next page with writing less code.

```
def parse(self, response):
    urls = response.xpath('//ul[@class="categories
    departments"]/li/a')

    for url in urls:
        yield response.follow(url, callback=self.parse_
        department_pages)
```

Here we use the syntactic sugar of Scrapy: under the hood the same code is executed, but you don't have to bother with extracting the exact reference from the anchor tags. And sometimes you don't get a fully qualified (absolute) URL in web page links but relative references, and you have to manually add the host (or use urljoin). By using response.follow you get this out of the box too. Therefore, I suggest you use this syntax, and I'll use this in the book too!

Currently, as of version 1.4.0, you have to provide a **single** URL or Link-type object to the follow method. I bet that someone will add a method that accepts a list (for example follow_all) too, because we like make things easier.

With this, we are done with this section. Let's move on and see how to get to the product pages.

At the end of this section, your basic.py file should look like this:

```
# -*- coding: utf-8 -*-
import scrapy

class BasicSpider(scrapy.Spider):
    name = 'basic'
    allowed_domains = ['www.sainsburys.co.uk']
    start_urls = ['https://www.sainsburys.co.uk/shop/gb/
    groceries/meat-fish/']

    def parse(self, response):
        urls = response.xpath('//ul[@class="categories
        departments"]/li/a')

        for url in urls:
            yield response.follow(url, callback=self.parse_
            department_pages)
```

Navigating Through Categories

Your first task is to navigate through the category pages of the Sainsbury's website. You have seen in the previous chapter how complex it can get to find the page where the item details are.

As you have seen in the previous chapter, each category's link can lead either to the product listing or to a page containing subcategories and their links, which can lead to either the product listing page or a third page with sub-subcategories. Fortunately, there is no deeper layering.

In this section we will handle the case wherin your code in the previous section resulted in a sub- or sub-subcategory page and not the product detail.

We sent requests with Scrapy in the previous section and told the tool to handle the responses with the parse_department_pages method.

To implement this method, we have to take care of the three versions of the response:

- We get a product listing page.

- We get a sub-category page.

- We get a sub-sub-category page.

If the response is a product listing, the idea is to forward the response to the next section's method. However, we must take care of triggering the requests. The resulting block will look like this one:

```
product_grid = response.xpath('//ul[@class="productLister
gridView"]')
    if product_grid:
        for product in self.handle_product_listings(response):
            yield product
```

In the preceding code, we call the handle_product_listings method with the response object. We could provide the product grid too (or just the grid) because we have it already extracted but, as you will see later, we need the response to navigate between the pages of the product grid.

Then we yield the result, which is the trigger for Scrapy to scrape these URLs too.

The next step is to get through the deeper layers of categories, which are represented by CSS classes like aisles (class="category aisles") and shelves (class="category shelves")–just like in your supermarket.

The trick here is to check if the page's source contains shelves and if not, then go for aisles. This is because a page containing shelves contains aisles too, and if you get the aisles links first you can end up in a never-ending circle of getting the same pages over and over again if you don't use caching. And getting the same pages means slower scraping (actually, never ending) and a lot of duplicate items in your scraping result.

```
pages = response.xpath('//ul[@class="categories shelf"]/li/a')
if not pages:
    pages = response.xpath('//ul[@class="categories aisles"]
    /li/a')
if not pages:
    # here is something fishy
    return

for url in pages:
    yield response.follow(url, callback=self.parse_department_
    pages)
```

The preceding code follows the approach mentioned previously: it looks for shelves and if they are not found, it looks for aisles. If nothing is found, then we are at a page from which we cannot gather more information: we have extracted the links to the product listings or there are no links to aisles or shelves on the page.

At the end of this section, your basic.py file should look something like this:

```
# -*- coding: utf-8 -*-
import scrapy

class BasicSpider(scrapy.Spider):
```

```
name = 'basic'
allowed_domains = ['www.sainsburys.co.uk']
start_urls = ['https://www.sainsburys.co.uk/shop/gb/
groceries/meat-fish/']

def parse(self, response):
    urls = response.xpath('//ul[@class="categories
    departments"]/li/a')

    for url in urls:
        yield response.follow(url, callback=self.parse_
        department_pages)

def parse_department_pages(self, response):
    product_grid = response.xpath('//ul[@class="product
    Lister gridView"]')
    if product_grid:
        for product in self.handle_product_listings
        (response):
            yield product

    pages = response.xpath('//ul[@class="categories
    shelf"]/li/a')
    if not pages:
        pages = response.xpath('//ul[@class="categories
        aisles"]/li/a')
    if not pages:
        # here is something fishy
        return

    for url in pages:
        yield response.follow(url, callback=self.parse_
        department_pages)
```

Navigating Through the Product Listings

Now your code leads at some point to a product listing page. In this section we will navigate through these pages if they have too many elements to display on one page, and we will request a download for the detailed item pages.

We are currently in the handle_product_listings function.

Let's start with the item details.

```
urls = response.xpath('//ul[@class="productLister gridView"]
//li[@class="gridItem"]//h3/a')
for url in urls:
    yield response.follow(url, callback=self.parse_product_detail)
```

The preceding code extracts the URLs to the detailed pages, and these URLs are then returned to the parse_department_pages method where their scraping is triggered.

```
next_page = response.xpath('//ul[@class="pages"]/li
[@class="next"]/a')
if next_page:
    yield response.follow(next_page, callback=self.handle_
    product_listings)
```

This code looks for the link to the next page. If one is found (on the website, it's under the > symbol) then it is returned to the parse_department_pages method. **Note** here the callback method: Because we know that we get another page of product listing, we can use the same method as a callback.

After finishing this section, your basic.py file should look like this:

```
# -*- coding: utf-8 -*-
import scrapy
```

```python
class BasicSpider(scrapy.Spider):
    name = 'basic'
    allowed_domains = ['www.sainsburys.co.uk']
    start_urls = ['https://www.sainsburys.co.uk/shop/gb/
    groceries/meat-fish/']

    def parse(self, response):
        urls = response.xpath('//ul[@class="categories
        departments"]/li/a')

        for url in urls:
            yield response.follow(url, callback=self.parse_
            department_pages)

    def parse_department_pages(self, response):
        product_grid = response.xpath('//ul[@
        class="productLister gridView"]')
        if product_grid:
            for product in self.handle_product_
            listings(response):
                yield product

        pages = response.xpath('//ul[@class="categories
        shelf"]/li/a')
        if not pages:
            pages = response.xpath('//ul[@class="categories
            aisles"]/li/a')
        if not pages:
            # here is something fishy
            return

        for url in pages:
            yield response.follow(url, callback=self.parse_
            department_pages)
```

```
def handle_product_listings(self, response):
    urls = response.xpath('//ul[@class="productLister
    gridView"]//li[@class="gridItem"]//h3/a')
    for url in urls:
        yield response.follow(url, callback=self.parse_
        product_detail)

    next_page = response.xpath('//ul[@class="pages"]/li
    [@class="next"]/a')
    if next_page:
        yield response.follow(next_page, callback=self.
        handle_product_listings)
```

Extracting the Data

Now that your code can handle the complex navigation and find the item details page, it's time to extract the required information from the website.

We are currently in the parse_product_detail method.

Now it is time to extract all the required information from the item page. Actually, this process is the same as you did in the previous chapter (if you coded along): you can use the queries; however, you can save some lines of code on validating every find or find_all call.

Without talking too much, let's jump into the code.

If you want, you can put down the book and implement the extraction logic. It is not hard, and you can use the information from the previous two chapters to go with.

My solution looks like this (yours may differ):

```
def parse_product_detail(self, response):
    product_name = response.xpath('//h1/text()').extract()[0].
    strip()
```

```python
product_image = response.urljoin(response.xpath('//div
[@id="productImageHolder"]/img/@src').extract()[0])

price_per_unit = response.xpath('//div[@
class="pricing"]/p[@class="pricePerUnit"]/text()').
extract()[0].strip()
units = response.xpath('//div[@class="pricing"]/span
[@class="pricePerUnitUnit"]').extract()
if units:
    unit = units[0].strip()

ratings = response.xpath('//label[@class="number
OfReviews"]/img/@alt').extract()
if ratings:
    rating = ratings[0]
reviews = response.xpath('//label[@class="number
OfReviews"]').extract()
if reviews:
    reviews = reviews_pattern.findall(reviews[0])
    if reviews:
        product_reviews = reviews[0]

item_code = item_code_pattern.findall(response.xpath('//p
[@class="itemCode"]/text()').extract()[0].strip())[0]

nutritions = {}
for row in response.xpath('//table[@class="nutrition
Table"]/tr'):
    th = row.xpath('./th/text()').extract()
    if not th:
        th = ['Energy kcal']
    td = row.xpath('./td[1]/text()').extract()[0]
    nutritions[th[0]] = td
```

```
product_origin = ' '.join(response.xpath(
    './/h3[@class="productDataItemHeader" and text()=
    "Country of Origin"]/following-sibling::div[1]/p/
    text()').extract())
```

And that is it. Extracting information on a product takes up to 30 lines of code (with my custom formatting settings). And this is just great!

As you can see in the code, there are some interesting code blocks. For example, every xpath call returns a list, even if you know there has to be at most one result. And some of those lists are empty because the product doesn't have ratings or unit information. As with Beautiful Soup, you must handle such cases with Scrapy too.

After this section, your basic.py file should look something like this:

```
# -*- coding: utf-8 -*-
import scrapy

reviews_pattern = re.compile("Reviews \((\d+)\)")
item_code_pattern = re.compile("Item code: (\d+)")

class BasicSpider(scrapy.Spider):
    name = 'basic'
    allowed_domains = ['www.sainsburys.co.uk']
    start_urls = ['https://www.sainsburys.co.uk/shop/gb/
    groceries/meat-fish/']

    def parse(self, response):
        urls = response.xpath('//ul[@class="categories
        departments"]/li/a')

        for url in urls:
            yield response.follow(url, callback=self.parse_
            department_pages)
```

```
def parse_department_pages(self, response):
    product_grid = response.xpath('//ul[@class="product
    Lister gridView"]')
    if product_grid:
        for product in self.handle_product_listings
        (response):
            yield product

    pages = response.xpath('//ul[@class="categories
    shelf"]/li/a')
    if not pages:
        pages = response.xpath('//ul[@class="categories
        aisles"]/li/a')
    if not pages:
        # here is something fishy
        return

    for url in pages:
        yield response.follow(url, callback=self.parse_
        department_pages)

def handle_product_listings(self, response):
    urls = response.xpath('//ul[@class="productLister
    gridView"]//li[@class="gridItem"]//h3/a')
    for url in urls:
        yield response.follow(url, callback=self.parse_
        product_detail)

    next_page = response.xpath('//ul[@class="pages"]/li[
    @class="next"]/a')
    if next_page:
        yield response.follow(next_page, callback=self.
        handle_product_listings)
```

121

```python
def parse_product_detail(self, response):
    product_name = response.xpath('//h1/text()').extract()
    [0].strip()
    product_image = response.urljoin(response.xpath('//
    div[@id="productImageHolder"]/img/@src').extract()[0])

    price_per_unit = response.xpath('//div[@
    class="pricing"]/p[@class="pricePerUnit"]/text()').
    extract()[0].strip()
    units = response.xpath('//div[@class="pricing"]/span
    [@class="pricePerUnitUnit"]').extract()
    if units:
        unit = units[0].strip()

    ratings = response.xpath('//label[@class="number
     OfReviews"]/img/@alt').extract()
    if ratings:
        rating = ratings[0]
    reviews = response.xpath('//label[@class="number
    OfReviews"]').extract()
    if reviews:
        reviews = reviews_pattern.findall(reviews[0])
        if reviews:
            product_reviews = reviews[0]

    item_code = item_code_pattern.findall(response.
    xpath('//p[@class="itemCode"]/text()').extract()[0].
    strip())[0]

    nutritions = {}
    for row in response.xpath('//table[@class="nutrition
    Table"]/tr'):
        th = row.xpath('./th/text()').extract()
```

```
    if not th:
        th = ['Energy kcal']
    td = row.xpath('./td[1]/text()').extract()[0]
    nutritions[th[0]] = td

product_origin = ' '.join(response.xpath(
    './/h3[@class="productDataItemHeader" and
    text()="Country of Origin"]/following-
    sibling::div[1]/p/text()').extract())
```

Where to Put the Data?

OK: you have followed along, implemented the product extractor, and you have a lot of variables in your spider that contain the information for the project, but where to store them?

With Scrapy, you have to store data in so-called *items*. These items are plain old Python classes and can be found in the items.py file. Besides this, these items behave as dictionaries: you declare them as Python classes and can fill them like dictionaries using a key-value assignment.

If you have run your spider after the previous step, you might have seen entries in the console like this one:

```
2018-02-11 11:06:03 [scrapy.extensions.logstats] INFO: Crawled
47 pages (at 47 pages/min), scraped 0 items (at 0 items/min)
```

Here you can see that there were no items scraped. We will fix this now.

Let's adapt the parse_product_detail method to put the data into an item. To do this, first of all we need an item, which is already there in the items.py file.

```
class SainsburysItem(scrapy.Item):
    # define the fields for your item here like:
    # name = scrapy.Field()
    pass
```

This class is currently empty; we must add fields to it. Because I don't like to write scrapy.Field() every time (even if it is just copy+paste), I like to do "static" imports (from scrapy import Item, Field).

My solution looks like this; yours may differ, depending on how you named your fields.

```
class SainsburysItem(Item):
    url = Field()
    product_name = Field()
    product_image = Field()
    price_per_unit = Field()
    unit = Field()
    rating = Field()
    product_reviews = Field()
    item_code = Field()
    nutritions = Field()
    product_origin = Field()
```

The only thing I changed is the nutritions field: I didn't add all the possible fields to the item definition. This makes writing the file easier and exporting to JSON (see later) more convenient.

A flat (a.k.a. all fields included) class would look like this:

```
class FlatSainsburysItem(Item):
    url = Field()
    product_name = Field()
    product_image = Field()
    price_per_unit = Field()
    unit = Field()
    rating = Field()
    product_reviews = Field()
    item_code = Field()
    product_origin = Field()
```

```
energy = Field()
energy_kj = Field()
kcal = Field()
fibre_g = Field()
carbohydrates_g = Field()
of_which_sugars = Field()
...
```

As you can see, the problem with this approach will come in the code: for the nutrition table you get strings as keys and you have to map them to these field names. This makes things complicated. Besides this, there are over *70* different fields that you must map.

I don't think it useful to include such mapping code here. If you are interested, you can give it a try, but it is not a requirement of this book or website scraping in general.

When we export the results to files later in this chapter, we will take a closer look at how fields containing dictionaries are exported by default and what we can do to get the same results as in Chapter 2.

Now to add and use items, you have to adapt the parse_product_ detail method like this:

```
def parse_product_detail(self, response):
    item = SainsburysItem()
    item['url'] = response.url
    item['product_name'] = response.xpath('//h1/text()').
    extract()[0].strip()
    item['product_image'] = response.urljoin(
        response.xpath('//div[@id="productImageHolder"]/img/
        @src').extract()[0])

    item['price_per_unit'] = response.xpath('//div[@class=
    "pricing"]/p[@class="pricePerUnit"]/text()').extract()
        [0].strip()
    units = response.xpath('//div[@class="pricing"]/span
    [@class="pricePerUnitUnit"]').extract()
```

```
    if units:
        item['unit'] = units[0].strip()

    ratings = response.xpath('//label[@class="number
    OfReviews"]/img/@alt').extract()
    if ratings:
        item['rating'] = ratings[0]
    reviews = response.xpath('//label[@class="number
    OfReviews"]').extract()
    if reviews:
        reviews = reviews_pattern.findall(reviews[0])
        if reviews:
            item['product_reviews'] = reviews[0]

    item['item_code'] = \
item_code_pattern.findall(response.xpath('//p[@class=
"itemCode"]/text()').extract()[0].strip())[0]

    nutritions = {}
    for row in response.xpath('//table[@class="nutrition
    Table"]/tr'):
        th = row.xpath('./th/text()').extract()
        if not th:
            th = ['Energy kcal']
        td = row.xpath('./td[1]/text()').extract()[0]
        nutritions[th[0]] = td
    item['nutritions'] = nutritions

    item['product_origin'] = ' '.join(response.xpath(
        './/h3[@class="productDataItemHeader" and
        text()="Country of Origin"]/following-
        sibling::div[1]/p/text()').extract())

    yield item
```

This involves defining the new item (add the import to the file: `from sainsburys.items import SainsburysItem`) and then use it like a dictionary. I used the variable names from the previous version as the `Field` names in my item definition, but it is up to you how to name your fields. You just must find the right mapping.

Finally, you must `yield` the item, which makes `Scrapy` know there's an item to handle.

The current state of the spider can be found in the folder `02_basic_spider` among the sources of this chapter.

Why Items?

Good question! Because items are dictionary-like objects; alternatively, you can use dictionaries to store your information.

```
item = {}
```

This doesn't result in any difference in coding or handling results, although `Scrapy`'s items hold some extended information that some components use. For example, exporters look at which fields to export, serialization can be customized by `Items` metadata, and you can use them to find memory leaks.

You will see later in this chapter that sometimes it is convenient to use a simple dictionary instead of an item. But for now, you should use items.

Running the Spider

Now it is time to start our spider, because we finished the extractor methods and added the items to export.

To start the spider, execute

```
scrapy crawl basic
```

from your crawler-projects main folder (where the scrapy.cfg file is located). In my case, this is

```
C:\wswp\chapter_4\sainsburys
```

Depending on your logging configuration, you either see something similar to this:

```
018-02-11 13:52:20 [scrapy.utils.log] INFO: Scrapy 1.5.0
started (bot: sainsburys)
2018-02-11 13:52:20 [scrapy.utils.log] INFO: Versions: lxml
4.1.1.0, libxml2 2.9.5, cssselect 1.0.3, parsel 1.4.0, w3lib
1.19.0, Twisted 17.9.0, Python 3.6.3 (v3.6.3:2c5fed8, Oct  3
2017, 18:11:49) [MSC v.1900 64 bit (AMD64)], pyOpenSSL 17.5.0
(OpenSSL 1.1.0g  2 Nov 2017), cryptography 2.1.4, Platform
Windows-10-10.0.16299-SP0
2018-02-11 13:52:20 [scrapy.crawler] INFO: Overridden settings:
{'BOT_NAME': 'sainsburys', 'CONCURRENT_REQUESTS': 1, 'LOG_
LEVEL': 'INFO', 'NEWSPIDER_MODULE': 'sainsburys.spiders',
'ROBOTSTXT_OBEY': True, 'SPIDER_MODULES': ['sainsburys.
spiders'], 'USER_AGENT': 'Mozilla/5.0 (Windows NT 10.0; Win64;
x64) AppleWebKit/537.36 (KHTML, like Gecko) Chrome/63.0.3239.84
Safari/537.36'}
2018-02-11 13:52:20 [scrapy.middleware] INFO: Enabled
extensions:
['scrapy.extensions.corestats.CoreStats',
 'scrapy.extensions.telnet.TelnetConsole',
 'scrapy.extensions.logstats.LogStats']
2018-02-11 13:52:20 [scrapy.middleware] INFO: Enabled
downloader middlewares:
['scrapy.downloadermiddlewares.robotstxt.RobotsTxtMiddleware',
 'scrapy.downloadermiddlewares.httpauth.HttpAuthMiddleware',
```

```
'scrapy.downloadermiddlewares.downloadtimeout.
DownloadTimeoutMiddleware',
'scrapy.downloadermiddlewares.defaultheaders.
DefaultHeadersMiddleware',
'scrapy.downloadermiddlewares.useragent.UserAgentMiddleware',
'scrapy.downloadermiddlewares.retry.RetryMiddleware',
'scrapy.downloadermiddlewares.redirect.MetaRefreshMiddleware',
'scrapy.downloadermiddlewares.httpcompression.
HttpCompressionMiddleware',
'scrapy.downloadermiddlewares.redirect.RedirectMiddleware',
'scrapy.downloadermiddlewares.cookies.CookiesMiddleware',
'scrapy.downloadermiddlewares.httpproxy.HttpProxyMiddleware',
'scrapy.downloadermiddlewares.stats.DownloaderStats']
2018-02-11 13:52:20 [scrapy.middleware] INFO: Enabled spider
middlewares:
['scrapy.spidermiddlewares.httperror.HttpErrorMiddleware',
'scrapy.spidermiddlewares.offsite.OffsiteMiddleware',
'scrapy.spidermiddlewares.referer.RefererMiddleware',
'scrapy.spidermiddlewares.urllength.UrlLengthMiddleware',
'scrapy.spidermiddlewares.depth.DepthMiddleware']
2018-02-11 13:52:20 [scrapy.middleware] INFO: Enabled item
pipelines:
[]
2018-02-11 13:52:20 [scrapy.core.engine] INFO: Spider opened
2018-02-11 13:52:20 [scrapy.extensions.logstats] INFO: Crawled
0 pages (at 0 pages/min), scraped 0 items (at 0 items/min)
2018-02-11 13:53:20 [scrapy.extensions.logstats] INFO: Crawled 220
pages (at 220 pages/min), scraped 205 items (at 205 items/min)
2018-02-11 13:54:20 [scrapy.extensions.logstats] INFO: Crawled 442
pages (at 222 pages/min), scraped 416 items (at 211 items/min)
```

```
2018-02-11 13:55:20 [scrapy.extensions.logstats] INFO: Crawled 666
pages (at 224 pages/min), scraped 630 items (at 214 items/min)
2018-02-11 13:56:20 [scrapy.extensions.logstats] INFO: Crawled 883
pages (at 217 pages/min), scraped 834 items (at 204 items/min)
...
2018-02-11 14:12:20 [scrapy.extensions.logstats] INFO: Crawled
4525 pages (at 257 pages/min), scraped 4329 items (at 246
items/min)
2018-02-11 14:13:01 [scrapy.core.engine] INFO: Closing spider
(finished)
2018-02-11 14:13:01 [scrapy.statscollectors] INFO: Dumping
Scrapy stats:
{'downloader/request_bytes': 11644228,
 'downloader/request_count': 4720,
 'downloader/request_method_count/GET': 4720,
 'downloader/response_bytes': 72337636,
 'downloader/response_count': 4720,
 'downloader/response_status_count/200': 4718,
 'downloader/response_status_count/302': 1,
 'downloader/response_status_count/404': 1,
 'finish_reason': 'finished',
 'finish_time': datetime.datetime(2018, 2, 11, 13, 13, 1, 337489),
 'item_scraped_count': 4515,
 'log_count/INFO': 27,
 'offsite/domains': 1,
 'offsite/filtered': 416,
 'request_depth_max': 13,
 'response_received_count': 4719,
 'scheduler/dequeued': 4719,
 'scheduler/dequeued/memory': 4719,
```

```
'scheduler/enqueued': 4719,
'scheduler/enqueued/memory': 4719,
'start_time': datetime.datetime(2018, 2, 11, 12, 52, 20,
860026)}
2018-02-11 14:13:01 [scrapy.core.engine] INFO: Spider closed
(finished)
```

or a lot more information buzzing through your screen. This is because of the default logging level. If you don't set it explicitly to INFO, you get all information Scrapy-developers thought useful. And one portion of this information is the item that was gathered. It is good to see on the console which items are processed, but for more than 3,000 entries this generates a lot of unwanted output.

These first lines of the prcedimg output tell you what configuration runs Scrapy. Here you can see the middlewares, pipelines, extensions, and all the important stuff to analyze if you encounter strange results.

```
2018-02-11 13:53:20 [scrapy.extensions.logstats] INFO: Crawled 220
pages (at 220 pages/min), scraped 205 items (at 205 items/min)
```

Over time, a new line like the preceding one pops up on the screen. This tells you the current progress: how many pages are scraped, how many items are extracted, and how fast the scraping is. These numbers vary on your settings: if you increase the concurrent requests and decrease the delay between requests, this will get faster (depending on the target website, of course). If you find such statistics annoying, you can disable them by adding the following to your spider's settings.py:

```
EXTENSIONS = {
    'scrapy.extensions.logstats.LogStats': None
}
```

When the scraping is done, you will see a similar summary to this:

```
2018-02-11 14:13:01 [scrapy.core.engine] INFO: Closing spider
(finished)
2018-02-11 14:13:01 [scrapy.statscollectors] INFO: Dumping
Scrapy stats:
{'downloader/request_bytes': 11644228,
 'downloader/request_count': 4720,
 'downloader/request_method_count/GET': 4720,
 'downloader/response_bytes': 72337636,
 'downloader/response_count': 4720,
 'downloader/response_status_count/200': 4718,
 'downloader/response_status_count/302': 1,
 'downloader/response_status_count/404': 1,
 'finish_reason': 'finished',
 'finish_time': datetime.datetime(2018, 2, 11, 13, 13, 1, 337489),
 'item_scraped_count': 4515,
 'log_count/INFO': 27,
 'offsite/domains': 1,
 'offsite/filtered': 416,
 'request_depth_max': 13,
 'response_received_count': 4719,
 'scheduler/dequeued': 4719,
 'scheduler/dequeued/memory': 4719,
 'scheduler/enqueued': 4719,
 'scheduler/enqueued/memory': 4719,
 'start_time': datetime.datetime(2018, 2, 11, 12, 52, 20, 860026)}
2018-02-11 14:13:01 [scrapy.core.engine] INFO: Spider closed
(finished)
```

In these statistic dumps you can find the summary of the whole scraping process: requests, errors, different HTTP codes, number of items scraped, memory usage, and many other useful things. This can give you ideas about where to enable extensions (for example finding which outside domains were triggered or which page wasn't found).

Download finished in 20 minutes. This is way better than the run using my basic scraper from Chapter 3 (I let it run prior to this run and it took 4,009 seconds). And we didn't have to write so much code.

Exporting the Results

Now you have the extracted data, you have the items representing the information, but the results are gone as soon as the spider finishes, and the Python process is gone from the memory of your computer.

Fortunately, Scrapy offers you built-in solutions, but they are very basic (you can call them primitive). But there's a way to plug in your custom solution and make the scraper behave.

In this section we will first explore the built-in options and see if they're really so primitive. Then we will take a look at how to shape the export to our needs—and yes, this requires writing some code.

Because Scrapy knows that scraping results in saving extracted information, it doesn't require you to configure the exporter pipeline. You can tell Scrapy to export the scraped results easily via the command-line using the -o option. From this, Scrapy will figure out what type of file you want to save if you provide the right file-extension (.csv for CSV, .json for JSON), or you can add the -t option too and tell in what format you want the data in your specified output file (the value provided with -t has to be a valid feed exporter—more on those later).

The only problem I encountered with these default exporters is that they **append** the results to the file: if the file doesn't exist, there's no problem. However, if the file exists and has contents (for example from a previous run) then the new data is simply appended to the file, resulting in invalid content.

Besides the JSON and CSV exporters I will discuss in the next section, you can export your items in XML, Pickle, or Marshal format. They are done with built-in item exporters and use already provided functionality.

133

To CSV

The first approach is to export everything to CSV. As you can see in the previous paragraph, you simply have to run the spider with the -o option providing a CSV file.

```
scrapy crawl basic -o sainsburys.csv
```

If the scraper is finished, you can open the sainsburys.csv file and look at its contents.

```
item_code,nutritions,price_per_unit,product_image,product_
name,product_origin,product_reviews,rating,unit,url
7906825,"{'Energy ': '762kJ/', 'Fat ': '9.8g', 'Saturates':
'3.5g', 'Carbohydrates': '6.6g', 'Sugars': '3.5g', 'Protein
': '16g', 'Salt ': '1.71g'}",£3.00,https://www.sainsburys.
co.uk/wcsstore7.25.53/ExtendedSitesCatalogAssetStore/images/
catalog/productImages/23/5060084344723/5060084344723_L.
jpeg,Black Farmer Reduced Fat Sausages 400g,,0,0.0,,https://
www.sainsburys.co.uk/shop/ProductDisplay?storeId=10151&product
Id=1200360&urlRequestType=Base&categoryId=352852&catalogId=1019
4&langId=44
```

Note   For Windows users, you may encounter extra blank lines in your file. This is because of a currently open bug in Scrapy but the main reason is in the line-ending differences between the operating systems. There's already a pull-request at GitHub[5] when I'm writing this; it has been merged and I hope it's available with the next released Scrapy version.

---

[5]https://github.com/scrapy/scrapy/pull/3039

Because each line has a lot of content, I don't want to list more here. But you can already see the interesting part: the nutrition column (in my example the second column). It has curly braces ({}) with the nutrition dictionary written out as text. This is not good; therefore, we will implement a custom item exporter to handle this case.

To JSON

Exporting to JSON works similar to CSV: you provide a JSON file as output.

```
scrapy crawl basic -o sainsburys.json
```

The result is a JSON file containing entries like this one:

```
{
  "url": "https://www.sainsburys.co.uk/shop/ProductDisplay?store
Id=10151&productId=1200360&urlRequestType=Base&categoryId=352
852&catalogId=10123&langId=44",
  "product_name": "Black Farmer Reduced Fat Sausages 400g",
  "product_image": "https://www.sainsburys.co.uk/
wcsstore7.25.53/ExtendedSitesCatalogAssetStore/images/
catalog/productImages/23/5060084344723/5060084344723_L.jpeg",
  "price_per_unit": "\u00a33.00",
  "rating": "0.0",
  "product_reviews": "0",
  "item_code": "7906825",
  "nutritions": {
    "Energy ": "762kJ/",
    "Fat ": "9.8g",
    "Saturates": "3.5g",
    "Carbohydrates": "6.6g",
    "Sugars": "3.5g",
    "Protein ": "16g",
```

```
    "Salt ": "1.71g"
  },
  "product_origin": ""
}
```

Using JSON, the `nutrition` dictionary fits great into the exported result. The keys could use a bit of tidying, but for now the structure looks great.

There's a little flaw in there: those nasty Unicode characters. To fix this, add the following line to your `settings.py` file:

```
FEED_EXPORT_ENCODING = 'utf-8'
```

After running the scraper again, the same entry looks like this:

```
{
  "url": "https://www.sainsburys.co.uk/shop/ProductDisplay?store
  Id=10151&productId=1200360&urlRequestType=Base&categoryId=276
  041&catalogId=10172&langId=44",
  "product_name": "Black Farmer Reduced Fat Sausages 400g",
  "product_image": "https://www.sainsburys.co.uk/
  wcsstore7.25.53/ExtendedSitesCatalogAssetStore/images/
  catalog/productImages/23/5060084344723/5060084344723_L.jpeg",
  "price_per_unit": "£3.00",
  "rating": "0.0",
  "product_reviews": "0",
  "item_code": "7906825",
  "nutritions": {
    "Energy ": "762kJ/",
    "Fat ": "9.8g",
    "Saturates": "3.5g",
    "Carbohydrates": "6.6g",
    "Sugars": "3.5g",
```

```
    "Protein ": "16g",
    "Salt ": "1.71g"
  },
  "product_origin": ""
}
```

As an alternative to whole JSON files, you can use JSON-lines. This format exports every item as a single JSON object, which enables handling a large amount of data because you don't have to load everything into memory and put it together into a megaobject to write to a file—or be read by your target platform.

Scrapy has a built-in exporter for this result type too, and you can access it with the following command:

```
scrapy crawl basic -o sainsburys.jl
```

If you look at your file system while running the spiders, you will see that JSON-lines files are written to the disk as soon as they're processed by the item pipelines! You don't have to wait till the scraping is done to get a valid file.

To Databases

Well, for databases there's no out of the box solution; you cannot add an extra parameter to the command line to write your results into a database.

If you want your data stored in a database, then you have to write your own solution. However, because storing in a database is a use-case I often encounter, I wanted to add it into this section and not in the next one when I write about bringing your own exporter.

We will take a look at two different types of databases: MongoDB and SQLite. They represent the approach to the majority of databases currently in use, although other cloud-based storage solutions are rising, but most of the clients are still using these types of databases.

MongoDB

First let's go and create the item pipeline.

```python
import pymongo

class MongoDBPipeline(object):

    def __init__(self, mongo_uri, mongo_db, collection_name):
        self.mongo_uri = mongo_uri
        self.mongo_db = mongo_db
        self.collection_name = collection_name

    @classmethod
    def from_crawler(cls, crawler):
        return cls(
            mongo_uri=crawler.settings.get('MONGO_URI'),
            mongo_db=crawler.settings.get('MONGO_DATABASE',
            'items'),
            collection_name=crawler.settings.get('MONGO_
            COLLECTION', 'sainsburys')
        )

    def open_spider(self, spider):
        self.client = pymongo.MongoClient(self.mongo_uri)
        self.db = self.client[self.mongo_db]

    def close_spider(self, spider):
        self.client.close()

    def process_item(self, item, spider):
        self.db[self.collection_name].insert_one(dict(item))
        return item
```

The idea while using any database is that you need a connection to the target database and **you must clean up** after you are finished. The pipeline above does this.

open_spider is called every time the spider is started, when the scrape starts. close_spider is called when the spider finishes its work and is dismissed. And these are the two methods where you have to *open* and *close* the connection to the database.

process_item processes the item, and in this case this item is stored in the database.

But the most interesting method is the from_crawler. If present, it has to return a new instance of the pipeline. The crawler provided to the method should be used to access the crawler-specific settings. In the case of the example, we get the connection, database, and collection settings–where the last two have default values and you don't have to provide them.

To have your pipeline working, you have to configure it in settings.py.

```
ITEM_PIPELINES = {
    'sainsburys.pipelines.MongoDBPipeline': 300
}
```

Then you need to provide the database configuration. You can do it either in the settings.py file (which makes the configuration hard-coded):

```
MONGO_URI = 'localhost:27017'
```

or you can provide it through the command line when starting the spider:

```
scrapy crawl basic -s MONGO_URI=localhost:27017
```

Because we're using pymongo, we don't even have to provide the database URI. In such cases, pymongo creates a default connection to localhost:27017.

After running the spider, we can see the results in the database, as shown in Figure 4-2.

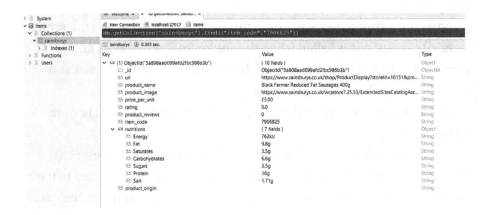

Figure 4-2. *The same item as previously–now in MongoDB*

You can find a spider using MongoDB to store the extracted information in the folder 03_mongodb among the sources for this chapter.

SQLite

Similar to the MongoDB solution, when using a SQLite database, you have to open and close the connection when the spider is started and finished, respectively.

Because handling the nutrition table gets too complex (with the 70 fields, which could be reduced), I won't implement this part of the export. If you're interested and want to give it a try, don't feel intimidated by my approach!

First, I defined the table DDL and the insert statement.

```
sqlite_ddl = """
CREATE TABLE IF NOT EXISTS {} (
    item_code INTEGER PRIMARY KEY,
    product_name TEXT NOT NULL,
    url TEXT NOT NULL,
    product_image TEXT,
    product_origin TEXT,
    price_per_unit TEXT,
    unit TEXT,
    product_reviews INTEGER,
    rating REAL
)
"""

sqlite_insert = """
INSERT OR REPLACE INTO {}
    values (?, ?, ?, ?, ?, ?, ?, ?, ?)
"""
```

Then I've written the code.

```
class SQLitePipeline:
    def __init__(self, database_location, table_name):
        self.database_location = database_location
        self.table_name = table_name
        self.db = None

    @classmethod
    def from_crawler(cls, crawler):
        return cls(
            database_location=crawler.settings.get('SQLITE_
            LOCATION'),
```

```python
            table_name=crawler.settings.get('SQLITE_TABLE',
            'sainsburys'),
        )

    def open_spider(self, spider):
        self.db = sqlite3.connect(self.database_location)
        self.db.execute(sqlite_ddl.format(self.table_name))

    def close_spider(self, spider):
        if self.db:
            self.db.close()

    def process_item(self, item, spider):
        if type(item) == SainsburysItem:
            self.db.execute(sqlite_insert.format(self.table_
            name),
                            (
                                item['item_code'],
                                item['product_name'],
                                item['url'], item['product_
                                image'],
                                item['product_origin'],
                                item['price_per_unit'],
                                item['unit'] if hasattr(item,
                                'unit') else None,
                                int(item['product_reviews'])
                                if hasattr(item, 'product_
                                reviews') else None,
                                float(item['rating']) if
                                hasattr(item, 'rating') else
                                None
                            )
                            )
        self.db.commit()
```

As you can see, the class works almost the same as the MongoDB pipeline from the previous example. The interesting part comes when you insert it into the database. Because we have some nullable fields (and properties that don't have to exist in the item), we have to ensure that we don't encounter a Python error while saving.

To test out the code, you have to add the pipeline to settings.py.

```
ITEM_PIPELINES = {
    'sainsburys.pipelines.MongoDBPipeline': None
    'sainsburys.pipelines.SQLitePipeline': 300
}
```

Now you can run the application.

```
scrapy crawl basic -s SQLITE_LOCATION=sainsburys.db
```

Don't forget to add the SQLite location with the -s settings flag. Without this you'll get an exception.

You can find a spider using SQLite to store the extracted information in the folder 04_sqlite among the sources for this chapter.

Bring Your Own Exporter

This section is the most interesting if you followed along and think the default exporting solution doesn't fit your needs.

Besides item pipelines (which we implemented for database connections), you can define your own feed exporters. These work like the built-in CSV, XML, and JSON exporters but adapted to your taste. In this section we will take a look at both approaches, even though you've already written two item pipelines for database storage.

You will now implement a CSV pipeline that will handle the nutritions field properly: instead of writing the whole dictionary as plain text, you will append the fields to the main content.

This requires you to store the extracted items in a cache just like with Beautiful Soup, because you cannot know the possible fields you may encounter in all the items. Remember: The website has multiple different nutrition tables that have more or less the same fields.

Filtering Duplicates

You remember the SQLite pipeline. There we defined INSERT OR REPLACE INTO when we saved an item into the database. This is because there are duplicate items that can be found from different pages on the website.

With SQLite you can easily overcome this problem, but with other exports you get too much data, and duplicates are never good. Sure, the postprocessing (your customer or data mining algorithm) can fix this, but why not you?

Because Scrapy is highly extensible, you will create a duplicate filter based on the item code.

```
from scrapy.exceptions import DropItem

class DuplicateItemFilter:
    def __init__(self):
        self.item_codes_seen = set()

    def process_item(self, item, spider):
        if item['item_code'] in self.item_codes_seen:
            raise DropItem("Duplicate item found: %s" %
            item['item_code'])

        self.item_codes_seen.add(item['item_code'])
        return item
```

The preceding code stores seen item codes in an internal set, and if the item code was seen already then it discards the item.

To enable this pipeline, add the following code to your settings.py file:

```
ITEM_PIPELINES {
    'sainsburys.pipelines.DuplicateItemFilter': 1
}
```

Setting a low value for the pipeline ensures that duplicates are filtered as soon as they arrive, saving a lot of work for other tasks.

And you can use such filter pipeline items for every possible kind of filtering. If you don't want an item to be present in the final export, then you can create a filter pipeline, add it to your settings.py, and it handles missing values.

Silently Dropping Items

If you add the item filter from the previous section and run your spider, you will see a lot of entries like this one:

```
2018-02-13 09:48:42 [scrapy.core.scraper] WARNING: Dropped:
Duplicate item found: 7887890
{'image_urls': ['https://www.sainsburys.co.uk/wcsstore7.25.53/
ExtendedSitesCatalogAssetStore/images/catalog/productImages/74/
0000000306874/0000000306874_L.jpeg'],
 'item_code': '7887890',
 'nutritions': {'Carbohydrate': '13.7g',
                'Energy': '664kJ',
                'Energy kcal': '158kcal',
                'Fat': '6.0g',
                'Fibre': '2.6g',
                'Mono-unsaturates': '3.5g',
                'Polyunsaturates': '1.5g',
```

```
                    'Protein': '11.1g',
                    'Salt': '0.91g',
                    'Saturates': '0.5g',
                    'Starch': '10.5g',
                    'Sugars': '3.2g'},
 'price_per_unit': '£2.50',
 'product_image': 'https://www.sainsburys.co.uk/
 wcsstore7.25.53/ExtendedSitesCatalogAssetStore/images/
 catalog/productImages/74/0000000306874/0000000306874_L.jpeg',
 'product_name': "Sainsbury's Mediterranean Tuna Fishcakes,
                    Taste the "
                    'Difference 300g',
 'product_origin': 'Produced in United Kingdom Produced using
                      Yellowfin tuna '
                      'caught by hooks and lines in the Western
                      Indian Ocean, '
                      'Eastern Indian Ocean, Western Central
                      Pacific Ocean and '
                      'Eastern Central Pacific Ocean',
 'product_reviews': '4',
 'rating': '2.0',
 'url': 'https://www.sainsburys.co.uk/shop/gb/groceries/all-
 fish-seafood/sainsburys-mediterranean-tuna-fishcakes--taste-
 the-difference-300g'}
```

One solution would be to raise the LOG_LEVEL to ERROR, but with this approach you end up skipping other warnings that can be useful in analyzing not expected behavior.

The other solution would be to write your own log-formatter for dropped items.

```
from scrapy import logformatter
import logging
```

```
class SilentlyDroppedFormatter(logformatter.LogFormatter):
    def dropped(self, item, exception, response, spider):
        return {
            'level': logging.DEBUG,
            'msg': logformatter.DROPPEDMSG,
            'args': {
                'exception': exception,
                'item': item,
            }
        }
```

To use this formatter, you must enable it in the settings.py file.

```
LOG_FORMATTER = 'sainsburys.formatter.SilentlyDroppedFormatter'
```

You can find a spider using the duplicate item filter in the folder
05_item_filter among the sources for this chapter.

Fixing the CSV File

Do you remember what problem the currently exported CSV files have?
Yes, they write the nutrition information as plain text into one column of
the CSV file. This is not ideal.

Besides this, the order of the columns may vary between runs because
they're stored in a dictionary.[6]

You will implement an item pipeline that stores every item during the
scraping process and exports only when the spider finishes.

---

[6]In the current version of Python, the dictionaries are ordered by their key per
default. This means every time you run your spider on the same 3.6 CPython
implementation, the order of the columns will stay the same.

147

```python
class CsvItemPipeline:

    def __init__(self, csv_filename):
        self.items = []
        self.csv_filename = csv_filename

    @classmethod
    def from_crawler(cls, crawler):
        return cls(
            csv_filename=crawler.settings.get('CSV_FILENAME',
            'sainsburys.csv'),
        )

    def open_spider(self, spider):
        pass

    def close_spider(self, spider):
        import csv
        with open(self.csv_filename, 'w', encoding='utf-8') as
        outfile:
            spamwriter = csv.DictWriter(outfile, fieldnames=self.
            get_fieldnames(), lineterminator='\n')
            spamwriter.writeheader()
            for item in self.items:
                spamwriter.writerow(item)

    def process_item(self, item, spider):
        if type(item) == SainsburysItem:
            new_item = dict(item)
            new_item.pop('nutritions')
            new_item.pop('image_urls')
            self.items.append({**new_item, **item['nutritions']})
        return item
```

```
def get_fieldnames(self):
    field_names = set()
    for product in self.items:
        field_names.update(product.keys())
    return field_names
```

You can see that every processed item is converted to a new dictionary that contains all the fields of the original item, then nutritions and image_urls are removed, finally the original nutritions dictionary is added to this new item by combining the two dictionaries, and the result is stored in memory for later usage.

When the spider finishes, all the different field names are extracted from all the items and are used as the CSV header. The order still varies between Python installations. To fix the order (at least for the standard properties that are not nutrition information) you can define a base list of properties and then add the missing values–something like this:

```
class CsvItemPipeline:
    fieldnames_standard = ['item_code', 'product_name',
    'url', 'price_per_unit', 'unit', 'rating', 'product_
    reviews','product_origin', 'product_image']

    def get_fieldnames(self):
        field_names = set()
        for product in self.items:
            for key in product.keys():
                if key not in self.fieldnames_standard:
                    field_names.add(key)
        return self.fieldnames_standard + list(field_names)
```

As always, you can add this pipeline to your settings.py file.

```
ITEM_PIPELINES = {
    'sainsburys.pipelines.CsvItemPipeline': 800,
}
```

However, using this approach, the CSV file will be written every time you run the spider, even if you export into a different format or don't want any export.

To solve this problem, let's implement a feed exporter.

You can find a spider using this CSV item pipeline in the folder 06_csv_pipeline among the sources for this chapter.

CSV Item Exporter

Feed exports are similar to item pipelines, but you can write them in a general fashion and use them on-demand, without changing the settings.py file.

You already used feed exporters (an alternative name for item exporters) when you saved information to CSV, JSON, or JSON-lines files using the -o output file and Scrapy could derive the exporter to use, or you can provide the -t option and tell Scrapy which exporter you want to use. The following list contains the currently built-in feed exporters:

- csv: saves information as CSV

- json: saves information as JSON

- jsonlines: saves information as JSON-lines

- xml: saves information as XML

- pickle: saves information as Pickle data

- marshal: saves information in Marshal format, which is similar to Pickle (specific to Python) but doesn't have any machine architectural issues

Because item exporters are similar to item pipelines, they process only one item at a time, we have to be tricky and save the items in memory just like for the CsvItemPipeline class. Basically, we will reuse the already written code and rename some methods.

```python
from scrapy.exporters import BaseItemExporter
import io
import csv

class CsvItemExporter(BaseItemExporter):
    fieldnames_standard = ['item_code', 'product_name', 'url',
    'price_per_unit', 'unit', 'rating', 'product_reviews',
                            'product_origin', 'product_image']

    def __init__(self, file, **kwargs):
        self._configure(kwargs)
        if not self.encoding:
            self.encoding = 'utf-8'

        self.file = io.TextIOWrapper(file,
                                        line_buffering=False,
                                        write_through=True,
                                        encoding=self.encoding)
        self.items = []

    def finish_exporting(self):
        spamwriter = csv.DictWriter(self.file,
         fieldnames=self.__get_fieldnames(),
         lineterminator='\n')
        spamwriter.writeheader()
        for item in self.items:
            spamwriter.writerow(item)

    def export_item(self, item):
        new_item = dict(item)
        new_item.pop('nutritions')
```

```
            new_item.pop('image_urls')
            self.items.append({**new_item, **item['nutritions']})

    def __get_fieldnames(self):
        field_names = set()
        for product in self.items:
            for key in product.keys():
                if key not in self.fieldnames_standard:
                    field_names.add(key)
        return self.fieldnames_standard + list(field_names)
```

But item exporters have a problem: they don't delete the file, they append to it. Fortunately, there is a solution: you can truncate the file to 0 bytes using the truncate() method. The extended constructor would look like this:

```
def __init__(self, file, **kwargs):
    self._configure(kwargs)
    if not self.encoding:
        self.encoding = 'utf-8'

    self.file = io.TextIOWrapper(file,
                                 line_buffering=False,
                                 write_through=True,
                                 encoding=self.encoding)
    self.file.truncate(0)
    self.items = []
```

And again, we must add the item exporter to the settings.py to let Scrapy know that there's another option you can use.

```
FEED_EXPORTERS = {
    'mycsv': 'sainsburys.exporters.CsvItemExporter'
}
```

Here you provided mycsv as the name of the feed exporter. This means, later you can call the spider using the -t option and mycsv as argument.

```
scrapy crawl basic -o mycsv.csv -t mycsv
```

You can find an example spider using the just-created feed exporter in the folder 07_csv_feed_exporter among the sources for this chapter.

Caching with Scrapy

Even though I think using caching is an advanced configuration option, I've added an extra section for this topic to cover. This is because it improves your execution time by multiple times, and once you cache the website locally you can tweak your scraper script as you wish without overloading the target server.

If you want to configure caching, for example while developing your scripts, there are some options in Scrapy. Naturally, you can write your own cache just like you did in the previous chapter but before you invest time, sweat, and brain cells into coding your cache, let's see what is present, what can we utilize.

Scrapy offers caching. The default configuration disables caching; this means, every page is downloaded every time you request it. But as you know, there are a lot of knobs you can turn, and you can enable caching with the HTTPCACHE_ENABLED = True setting.

There are three HTTP cache options you can utilize out of the box:

- File system storage
- DBM storage
- LevelDB storage

And as always, you can write your own solution too; however, I consider this scenario unlikely, because 90% of use-cases can be covered with the built-in solutions.

My **default** caching configuration looks like this:

```
HTTPCACHE_ENABLED = True
HTTPCACHE_EXPIRATION_SECS = 0
HTTPCACHE_DIR = 'httpcache'
HTTPCACHE_IGNORE_HTTP_CODES = []
```

With this you can enable caching, and when you run your spider it stores every request-response pair on your file system in the .scrapy/ httpcache folder in your project's directory, and from now on it uses this cache when you rerun your spider. This is ideal for tweaking your script: download a snapshot of the target website and use it for fine-tuning your item extraction.

If you have any HTTP response codes that you don't want cached, you can add them in the HTTPCACHE_IGNORE_HTTP_CODES list, for example:

```
HTTPCACHE_IGNORE_HTTP_CODES = [503, 418]
```

Setting HTTPCACHE_EXPIRATION_SECS to 0 keeps files always in the cache. If you give it a positive value, older cached files are discarded. **Note** that this setting requires values in seconds!

Let's see what caching has to offer!

Storage Solutions

In this section we will look at the different storage solutions Scrapy has to offer for caching. Out of the box you have the following options available:

- File System Storage

- DBM Storage

- LevelDB Storage

But because you can extend Scrapy easily, you can write your own storage solution (for example to use a custom database, like MongoDB).

If you ask me, I am fine with a file system–based solution. However, if you're running on-demand (for example in the cloud or in a container environment), you may favor a remote caching service, which is most likely based on a database.

File System Storage

If you enable HTTP caching, this is the default solution used. Even though it's the default, you can add the following line to your settings.py file:

```
HTTPCACHE_STORAGE = 'scrapy.extensions.httpcache.
                     FilesystemCacheStorage'
```

Using this storage option, all requests and responses are downloaded and stored in a folder whose name is unique for this scraper and is 40 characters long. In these folders is all the information identifying the request and the response the middleware will need to identify pages that should be served from the cache.

DBM Storage

To activate the DBM[7]storage, just add (or replace if it exists).

```
HTTPCACHE_STORAGE = 'scrapy.extensions.httpcache.
                     DbmCacheStorage'
```

The default setting is to use the anydbm module, but you can change it using the HTTPCACHE_DBM_MODULE setting.

---

[7]https://en.wikipedia.org/wiki/Dbm

LevelDB Storage

You can also use LevelDB[8] (a fast key-value storage) for your cache, but it is not encouraged in the development phase of your project because it allows only a single process to access the database at the same time. This is OK if you just run your spider, but if you want to have the Scrapy shell open for your project and run the spider you will end up with an error.

To use LevelDB you can change the HTTPCACHE_STORAGE to 'scrapy. extensions.httpcache.LeveldbCacheStorage' in the settings.py file and install LevelDB with the following command:

```
pip install leveldb
```

Cache Policies

Scrapy comes with two default policies for caching:

- Dummy policy
- RFC2616 policy

Dummy Policy

The *Dummy policy* is the default setting. Here, every request and its response are stored, and when the same request is seen again, the stored response is returned. This is useful if you are testing your spider and want to replay runs at the same.

Because this is the default policy, you don't have to add anything to your project's settings.py file.

---

[8]https://github.com/google/leveldb

RFC2616 Policy

This policy is aware of cache-control settings and is aimed at production use to avoid downloading unchanged pages, save bandwidth, and speed-up crawls.

To enable this policy, add the following setting to your settings.py file:

```
HTTPCACHE_POLICY = scrapy.extensions.httpcache.RFC2616Policy
```

What does **aware of cache-control settings** mean? It means that the scraper works according to the RFC2616 caching specification. If you are lazy and don't want to read the whole specification, here is a small excerpt of what Scrapy can do for you:

- If the website provides a no-store response, Scrapy won't try to store requests or responses.

- If the no-cache directive is set, Scrapy won't return the response from the cache, even it is downloaded recently.

- It computes the current age from the Age or the Date headers.

- It computes the freshness lifetime from the max-age directive, the Expires, and the Last-Modified response headers.

However, when writing this book, some RFC2616 compliance requirements are not met, such as:

- Pragma: no-cache support

- Vary header support

- Invalidation after updates or deletes

157

Downloading Images

Even though this is not a requirement for our project, you will encounter many tasks where you must download images besides data. Fortunately, Scrapy has a built-in solution for this problem too.

For this section, let's extend our requirements to gather images along with the items. These images will be saved on your file system besides your project files, but you can configure your spider to store the downloaded files at Amazon S3 or Google Cloud.

Because Scrapy uses Pillow for image resizing and thumbnail generation, you must install it before you can start gathering images.

```
pip install pillow
```

To get started, first add the following to your settings.py file:

```
ITEM_PIPELINES = {
    'scrapy.pipelines.images.ImagesPipeline': 5
}
```

And you have to tell Scrapy where to save the downloaded images. I use the images folder inside the project.

```
IMAGES_STORE = 'images'
```

The folder you provide to IMAGES_STORE must exist.

The combination of those two settings activates the image pipeline, which downloads the files and stores them on your computer's hard disk.

To get items into this pipeline, you must add

```
image_urls = Field()
images = Field()
```

to your Item. This is because the ImagesPipeline works using the image_urls field and adds the resulting images to the images field.

In the case of the Sainsbury's scraper, we must rename product_image to image_urls, add images in the SainsburysItem, and change the spider code to fill image_urls with a list instead of a URL.

```
item['image_urls'] = [response.urljoin(
response.xpath('//div[@id="productImageHolder"]/img/@src').
extract()[0])]
```

Now if you run your spider and save the results (for example using scrapy crawl basic -o images.jl), you will see the downloaded images in the images/full folder, similar to the one shown in Figure 4-3.

▸Name	Ext
📁 [..]	
01554ca3924bd70f2564ef51b9ef9873084b8b8c	jpg
01c8eb751d4fc0f35da6497bb7a19e72bbb1484d	jpg
024ef67b6ba3d13c9a81815b4a761fe92f474760	jpg
0258c6884eaa2199dd53f80e400ac9b782ea842d	jpg
026308dc6fe278a39b810d87dd6790163d3c23b3	jpg
0314ab1317a2600cb4ed191064e94660482783c9	jpg
03f4f9c000bf8aa753d06304b169ece4b8b4f1c8	jpg
040676510238bac65e621ae4168d292296075197	jpg
041c61322681b47ed4591f11f9de8e9f1fb028e1	jpg
0433aa23e7e71ff6a9ca5da8c87beefed29f283e	jpg
04851a3c7abc3171b4bcfa8a2eb4925e7ca0d184	jpg
05014cf44ea1275204c2c8c744e238544f6fd37b	jpg
05107856d6203c135b2eebe318a42558d9867493	jpg
056fcd928588581da576ba3ebbcff83a790ef5bf	jpg
057e32749e676a0f2683691c4f0d922770a25c93	jpg
058c4bc619d9f7e81fe5edb0ec9b0f20b88b5215	jpg
06bbb21e9c4e4887ad44f2391bbed36e9811e05f	jpg
06d0c073bfdc917e058bf9f3a7f2e6892726ef49	jpg
0737393d450d5475b744081b32ffe31e5a082c6b	jpg
074e003c95181c516e63f534808c36eb1f9ce500	jpg
074e0db6681d2b78d900d02025d13912e64916c0	jpg
08429e7b75560bd62ecd0fdd8c42cd57ed597bcd	jpg
085b3c1465669b6d34631efa35ad0a76c44c9a40	jpg
0862a0807d8c2e3ac604226d0b556945d1efebe8	jpg
08cb661734cf8db220a3d10961d09c157891f6bb	jpg
096f7a3551780bb35da78bd72dae9234f382da5d	jpg
0982299bb2ec5d06b0c1eaec27b961ad89039a6c	jpg

Figure 4-3. *Images downloaded when Scrapy ran*

159

The values in the `images.jl` file are inserted into the item's `images` field. A sample value looks like this:

```
"images": [
    {
        "url": "https://www.sainsburys.co.uk/wcsstore7.25.53/
        ExtendedSitesCatalogAssetStore/images/catalog/product
        Images/23/5060084344723/5060084344723_L.jpeg",
        "path": "full/4ae5a3a0dfa0fac7f3728d76b788716e8a2bc9fb.jpg",
        "checksum": "132512348d379f8365ca02082a16adf1"
    }
]
```

This tells you not only how the file is named on your file system and where it's downloaded from, but you get a checksum too to verify that the image on your file system is really the same that Scrapy downloaded.

In the preceding example, the file can be found under `images/full/4ae5a3a0dfa0fac7f3728d76b788716e8a2bc9fb.jpg` and is shown in Figure 4-4.

Note   You can find the sources for this section in the `08_image_pipeline` folder among the sources for this chapter.

Figure 4-4. *An example of a downloaded image*

Scrapy uses its own algorithm to generate the file names. This means you can encounter different file names than me if you run the spider on your computer.

Using **Beautiful Soup** with **Scrapy**

Sometimes you already have an HTML extractor ready, created with Beautiful Soup, and you don't want to convert it to Scrapy code. Or you have a team member who is a pro at Beautiful Soup and she creates the extraction code; you only have to take care of configuring Scrapy.

In such cases you use the already existing code because you can integrate Beautiful Soup and Scrapy.

```
def parse_product_details_bs(self, response):
    item = SainsburysItem()

    from bs4 import BeautifulSoup
    soup = BeautifulSoup(response.text, 'lxml')
    h1 = soup.find('h1')
    if h1:
        item['product_name'] = h1.text.strip()
```

In the preceding code you can see the integration of Beautiful Soup and Scrapy with a subset of the code from the previous chapter. I explicitly use lxml for speed while parsing but you can use any of the available parsers (and by the way, lxml is available out of the box when you install Scrapy).

With this information, you can rewrite the spider to use the functionality written in Chapter 3. You can find a sample solution in the 09_beautifulsoup folder among the sources for this chapter.

Logging

Sometimes you prefer to see custom messages in the console while scraping. This is useful if you cut back the log level of Scrapy to INFO but you want to see a little more of the current process.

Every spider comes with a logger, which you can access right in its methods. For example, logging the response's URL would look like this:

```
self.logger.info("URL: %s", response.url)
```

The logger uses the same log levels that you configured in settings.py. If you don't see a log output on the console, you can turn up the logging (decrease the level to DEBUG). If it still doesn't show up, then you can be sure that the code is not reached while running.

If you want to do standard logging and not use the logger in your spider (for example because you are in a different file where you don't have access to a spider), you can either use Scrapy's log module (which is deprecated so you shouldn't use it) or Python's built-in logger module. There are no considerations; logger works the same way as it would in a "standard" Python application.

(A Bit) Advanced Configuration

Because there are a lot of knobs you can turn on your Scrapy project, I add a section to get you started and try out some different combinations.

This book has size limitations; therefore, I won't list every setting you can toggle, but just the most used ones. For more settings, take a look at Scrapy's documentation: https://doc.scrapy.org.

LOG_LEVEL

Working through this chapter gave you a lot of output while running the spider. However, you can restrict the information to a subset.

As a default, Scrapy uses the DEBUG log-level for its output. It logs you every bit of information you can get from the code, and most of the time this is too much.

However, you can restrict the log level in the settings.py file by adding the following line:

```
LOG_LEVEL = 'INFO'
```

This sets the log level to log only information, and warning and error messages. This is because of how logging levels work. Each has a priority, and with the log level setting you tell the application to "log the items with this priority and above."

You can use the following list as a reference to the log-level priority:

1. CRITICAL

2. ERROR

3. WARNING

4. INFO

5. DEBUG

This list contains Scrapy's log level settings. DEBUG is a good setting while developing, but in a running/live system I prefer INFO or sometimes WARNING as the log level. Depending on the developer, you get the right amount of information using this level.

CONCURRENT_REQUESTS

You have already seen this setting at the beginning of this chapter. As its name already tells you, you can limit the number of concurrent requests to one website.

Depending on the website, it makes sense to turn this number up a bit or stay with the default value. This is because network operations (downloading the website's code) take time, and while the thread waits the process/application is hanging idle. In such cases, even with the GIL present, Python can execute multiple threads parallel, and therefore while your code is waiting for one page to load you can download more.

However, you cannot turn the knob forever. Your computer has its limits too, and having 16 or 160 concurrent requests doesn't make a difference. I suggest you start with 1 request while developing, then use the default setting of 16. This is good for you because you get the required data faster, and this is good for the targeted website too because it's not overwhelmed by you.

Moreover, sometimes it happens that the target website has request monitoring enabled. This means, requests and their interval are monitored and evaluated, and if your IP exceeds a threshold you get banned for a time from the website—sometimes forever. Therefore, be responsible with your configuration.

DOWNLOAD_DELAY

Accompanying the concurrent requests, you can set the delay between two downloads too. The download delay tells the spider how many seconds it should wait between downloading another page from the same domain or IP address (if CONCURRENT_REQUESTS_PER_IP is set to a nonzero positive number).

This configuration awaits seconds as value, but you can provide decimal values too.

```
DOWNLOAD_DELAY = 0.125 # 125 milliseconds
```

This setting is used to not hit the target servers too hard with your requests. Sometimes this setting is useful to avoid detection and mock human-like behavior.

Autothrottling

Previously, you have seen how to set hard download delays and concurrent requests, to act like a good citizen. However, with this approach you can end up with many requests waiting for completion if the server is busy. Or if the server starts to send back error messages, those are returned faster than 200 OK responses, which generate more requests per second because errors are handled faster by Scrapy. However, in case of errors, the scraper should send fewer requests to help the server to recover itself from its (hopefully temporary) failure state.

A solution, and an alternative approach, is to use Scrapy's autothrottling feature. This is not enabled by default; you must enable it with the following setting:

```
AUTOTHROTTLE_ENABLED = True
```

What the algorithm behind this setting does is adjust the download delay based on the response times of the server. If the server is busy, it sends the responses later, and Scrapy adjusts the download delay to send requests less frequently. If the server has no difficulties, the download delay is reduced, and more requests are sent to the server. And most importantly: non-200-OK responses do not decrease the download delay.

You can configure some settings for autothrottling too. For example, setting

```
AUTOTHROTTLE_START_DELAY = 15
```

You tell Scrapy to wait 15 seconds initially between two requests. Based on the server's response time, Scrapy can reduce or extend this waiting time. If the latency is big, Scrapy raises this delay. However, you can give it a maximum where it won't wait longer.

```
AUTOTHROTTLE_MAX_DELAY = 25
```

This setting tells Scrapy to wait at most 25 seconds until the next request.

To have detailed information on all the requests and their responses, you can enable debugging for auto-throttling.

```
AUTOTHROTTLE_DEBUG = True
```

COOKIES_ENABLED

You know cookies. They are settings stored in your browser and exchanged by every request with the server. They store information regarding your session, browsing preferences, or settings at the website. Sometimes they are required to prove you are using a browser. Sometimes you have to avoid a subset, because they tell the server you're not using a browser. If you're browsing in the European Union (EU), you get a notification about cookies by visiting almost every EU website. This is quite annoying, but a regulation to be aware of that websites store (let store) information about your browsing history.

As you may think, sometimes it is required to use cookies (for example websites that require login), but sometimes it's better to avoid them.

The default setting in Scrapy is to use cookies. This means that every time the target web server returns an HTTP parameter Set-Cookie its value is stored internally by Scrapy and is sent back to the server with every new request.

You can disable this setting by adding the following configuration to your settings.py file:

```
COOKIES_ENABLED = False
```

If you want to debug which cookies are exchanged between the server and your spider, you can add the following configuration:

```
COOKIES_DEBUG = True
```

This will log every sent cookie (the `Cookie` header in your request) and received cookie (the `Set-Cookie` header in the response) to the console, or the logging framework you specified.

Summary

In this chapter you learned about `Scrapy`, the tool for website scraping. You implemented the scraper for the requirements of Chapter 2 with `Scrapy`. You have seen that you need to write much less than when you use a homemade spider where you have to handle requests–just to mention one example.

You learned some advanced topics too like writing your own middleware, pipelines, and extensions, and what the result is if you turn some knobs on the configuration panel.

Now you are a full-fledged website scraper. You have the tools with which you can complete 75% of all scraping jobs. Feel free to stop reading here, but keep in mind that these 75% are decreasing with the emerging number of JavaScript-heavy websites that render data dynamically.

The next chapter will cover an advanced topic I rarely use: handling web pages with JavaScript. There are different approaches, and we will go a bit deeper because I will show you options other than Selenium. If you are interested in the "Why?," keep on reading!

CHAPTER 5

Handling JavaScript

This chapter is all about handling websites that utilize JavaScript to render information dynamically.

You have seen in the previous chapters that a basic website scraper loads the web page's contents and does its extraction on this source code. And if there's JavaScript included, it's not executed, and the dynamic information is missing from the page.

This is bad, at least in those cases where you need that dynamic data.

Another interesting part of scraping websites that use JavaScript is that you may need clicks or button presses to go to the right page / get the right content, because these actions call a chain of JavaScript functions.

Now I will give you options for how you can deal with these problems. Most of the time you will find *Selenium* as the solution, if you Google or search the Internet with other engines. However, there are other options present, and I will give you more insight. Perhaps those other options will fit your needs better.

Reverse Engineering

This first option is for advanced developers–at least I feel advanced developers will do more reverse engineering.

The idea here is to use the DevTools from Chrome (or similar functionality in other browsers), enable JavaScript, and monitor the XHR network flow to find out which data is requested from the server and rendered separately.

© Gábor László Hajba 2018
G. L. Hajba, *Website Scraping with Python*, https://doi.org/10.1007/978-1-4842-3925-4_5

With the target endpoint (either a GET or a POST request) in your hands, you see which parameters to provide and how they affect the results.

Let's look at a simple example: at kayak.com you can search for flights and, therefore, airports too. In this simple example we will reverse engineer the destination search endpoint to extract some information, even if this information is not valuable.

I'll use Chrome for these examples. This is because I use Chrome for all my scraping tasks. It will work with Firefox too, if you know how to handle the developer tools.

First let's go to kayak.com, open up the DevTools window, and locate the *Network* tab there, as shown in Figure 5-1.

Figure 5-1. *Kayak.com with DevTools open*

As you can see in the image, I already navigated to the *XHR* tab inside the *Network* tab because all AJAX and XHR calls are listed here.

Now let's click the field on the website labeled **To?** and type in a letter, for example S, and watch the values on the right side inside the *XHR* tab, as shown in Figure 5-2.

Figure 5-2. *A small list of airports*

Now you get a list of some possible airports on the website, but two XHR requests too. We're interested in the request starting with `marvel`:

`www.kayak.com/mv/marvel?f=h&where=so&s=50&lc_cc=US&lc=en&v=v2&cv=5.`

This is the request that returns the information about the airport. It has some parameters where I have no idea what they do and how the results are affected if changed, but here's what I know:

- `where` is the key you're searching for

- `s` is the type of the search; 58 is for airports

- `lc` is the locale; you can change it and get different results—more on this later

- `v` is the version; there's a small difference in the result format if you choose `v1` instead of the default `v2`

Based on this information, what can we get out of it? We get some airports, and some idea about how to reverse engineer JavaScript and when to decide to use a different tool.

In this example, the JavaScript rendering is a simple HTTP GET call—nothing fancy, and I bet you already have an idea how to extract information delivered from these endpoints. Yes, using either the `requests` and Beautiful Soup libraries or Scrapy and some `Request` objects.

Back to the example: when you vary the lc value, for example, to de or es in the request, you get back different airports and the description of these airports in the locale you chose. This means JavaScript reverse engineering is not just about finding the right calls you want to use but also requires a bit of thinking.

Thoughts on Reverse Engineering

If you find yourself having a search that utilizes an HTTP endpoint to get the data, you can try to figure out how the search works. For example, instead of sending some values you expect to deliver results, try to add search expressions. Such expressions could be * to match all, .+ to evaluate regular expressions, or % if it has some kind of SQL query in the back.

Summary

You see, sometimes JavaScript reverse engineering pays off: you learned that those nasty XHR calls are simple requests and you can cover them from your scripts. However, sometimes JavaScript makes more complex things like rendering and loading data after the initial page is loaded. And you don't want to reverse engineer this, believe me.

Splash

Splash[1] is an open-source JavaScript rendering engine written in Python. It is lightweight and has a smooth integration with Scrapy.

It is maintained, and new versions are released every few months, when need arises.

---

[1]https://splash.readthedocs.io/en/stable/

Set-up

The basic and easiest usage of Splash is getting a Docker image from the developers and running it. This ensures that you have all the dependencies required by the project and can start using it. In this section we will use Docker.

To get started, install Docker if you don't have it already. You can find more information on installing Docker here: `https://docs.docker.com/manuals/`.

If this is done, you can get the image executing the following commands on your console:

```
docker pull scrapinghub/splash
docker run -p 5023:5023 -p 8050:8050 -p 8051:8051
scrapinghub/splash
```

Note   On some machines, administrator rights are required to start Splash. For example, on my Windows 10 computer, I had to run the docker container from an administrator console. On Unix-like machines, you may need to run the container using `sudo`.

Now Splash is running on localhost:8050, and it should look something like Figure 5-3.

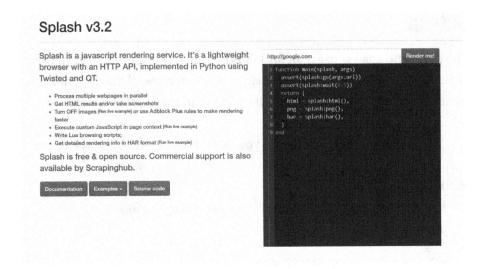

Figure 5-3. *Splash welcome screen*

Now you can enter a URL at the top right corner and hit `Render me!` to get the website rendered. If you input `http://sainsburys.co.uk` you get a similar result to the one shown in Figure 5-4 (the image will vary).

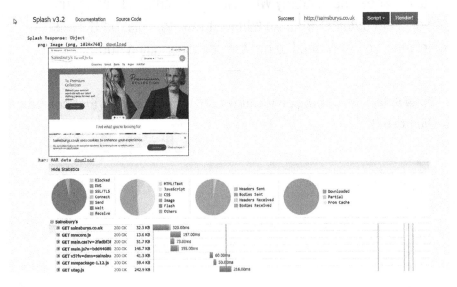

Figure 5-4. *Splash rendered Sainsbury's*

As you can see, you get a screenshot from the page you are scraping, and below it some statistics and timing of the requests rendering the website involved. At the bottom of the page you see the source code of the website, as shown in Figure 5-5.

Figure 5-5. *Splash with sources*

This source code is the one you get after the page is rendered. To verify this, you can open an interactive Python shell and get the website using requests.

```
>>> import requests
>>> r = requests.get('http://sainsburys.co.uk')
>>> r.text
'<!DOCTYPE html><html class="no-js" lang="en"><head><meta
charset="utf-8"><title>Sainsbury\'s</title><meta
name="description" content="Shop online at Sainsbury\'s
for everything from groceries and clothing to homewares,
electricals and more. We also offer a great range of
financial services. Live well for less."><meta name="viewport"
```

```
content="width=device-width,initial-scale=1"><meta
name="google-site-verification" content="soOzMsGig7xqxpwJQWd8qJ
kf0QQvLOj-ZS9fI9eSDiE"><link rel="shortcut icon" href="favicon.
ico"><meta http-equiv="X-UA-Compatible" content="IE=edge,
chrome=IE8"><script type="text/javascript" src="//service.
maxymiser.net/cdn/sainsburyscoUK/js/mmcore.js"></script>
<!--[if lt IE 9]>\n    <script src="https://cdn.polyfill.io/
v1/polyfill.min.js"></script>\n    <link rel="stylesheet"
href="homepage/css/main_ie8.css?v=65f0de0508c75d5aac750158
0ddf4e0a">\n    <![endif]--><!--[if gte IE 9]>\n    <link
rel="stylesheet" href="homepage/css/main.css?v=2fadbf3f7bf0aa
1b5e3613ec61ebabf7">\n    <![endif]--><link rel="stylesheet"
href="homepage/css/main.css?v=2fadbf3f7bf0aa1b5e3613ec61eba
bf7"><!--[if !IE]><!--><!--<![endif]--></head><body><script
type="text/javascript">(function(a,b,c,d)
....
```

The preceding example result is just an excerpt. If you save this code into an HTML file and open it in a browser and do the same with the sources returned by Splash, you will see the same page. The difference is in the sources: Splash has more lines and contains expanded JavaScript functions.

A Dynamic Example

To see how to get Splash working with dynamic websites (which utilize JavaScript a lot), let's see a different example. For instance, http://www.protopage.com/ generates you a web page based on a prototype, which you can customize. If you visit the site, you must wait some seconds until the page gets rendered.

If we want to scrape data from this site (there's not much available either, but imagine it has a lot to offer) and we use a simple tool (the requests library, Scrapy) or Splash with the default settings, we only get the base page that tells us that the page is currently rendered.

To have the rendered site rendered with Splash, I altered the script (which is written in Lua by the way) and turned up the wait time to **three seconds**.

```
function main(splash, args)
  assert(splash:go(args.url))
  assert(splash:wait(3))
  return {
    html = splash:html(),
    png = splash:png(),
    har = splash:har(),
  }
end
```

Depending on the network speed and load on the target website, three seconds can be too short. Feel free to experiment with different values for your target websites to have the page rendered.

Now all this is good, but how to use Splash to scrape websites?

Integration with Scrapy

The recommended way by Splash developers is to integrate this tool with Scrapy, and because we use Scrapy as our scraping tool, we will take a thorough look at how it can be accomplished.

First, we need to install the Splash Python package using pip.

```
pip install scrapy-splash
```

Now that this library is installed, we need to enable the middlewares that have been delivered with `scrapy-splash`.

```
DOWNLOADER_MIDDLEWARES = {
    'scrapy_splash.SplashCookiesMiddleware': 720,
    'scrapy_splash.SplashMiddleware': 725,
'scrapy.downloadermiddlewares.httpcompression.Http
CompressionMiddleware': 810,
}
```

The prceding numbers are not fully empiric: the Splash middlewares must have a higher order than the `HttpProxyMiddleware`, which has a default value of 750. To be on the safe side (for example Scrapy changes the default value of this proxy middleware), we could alter the middleware configuration like this:

```
DOWNLOADER_MIDDLEWARES = {
    'scrapy_splash.SplashCookiesMiddleware': 720,
    'scrapy_splash.SplashMiddleware': 725,
'scrapy.downloadermiddlewares.httpproxy.HttpProxyMiddleware': 750,
'scrapy.downloadermiddlewares.httpcompression.
HttpCompressionMiddleware': 810,
}
```

Then we must add the spider middleware to save disk space and network traffic. This is optional; if you don't do this, duplicate Splash arguments are stored on your disk and sent to your Splash server (this will be interesting in the Cloud–see next chapter for more on that topic).

```
SPIDER_MIDDLEWARES = {
    'scrapy_splash.SplashDeduplicateArgsMiddleware': 100,
}
```

Now we can define some variables required for Splash to work. One of these is the SPLASH_URL, which (obviously) tells the middleware where your Splash instance is available for rendering.

```
SPLASH_URL = 'http://localhost:8050/'
```

The next two variables come because Scrapy doesn't provide a way to override request fingerprints, and this makes routing those requests and responses between your script and Splash a bit complicated. However, the developers of Splash came up with a solution and you can use their configuration.

```
DUPEFILTER_CLASS = 'scrapy_splash.SplashAwareDupeFilter'
HTTPCACHE_STORAGE = 'scrapy_splash.SplashAwareFSCacheStorage'
```

The second variable points to a cache storage solution, which is aware of Splash. If you're using another custom cache storage, you must adapt it to work with Splash. This requires you to subclass the aforementioned storage class and replace all calls to scrapy.util.request.request_fingerprint with scrapy_splash.splash_request_fingerprint to have those nasty changed fingerprints work out.

The last change we must adapt is the usage of Requests: instead of using the default Scrapy Request we need to use SplashRequest.

Now let's adapt the Sainsbury's spider to use Splash.

Adapting the **basic** Spider

In an ideal world, you would only need to alter the configuration as we did in the previous section, and all requests and responses would go over Splash because we don't have any usages of Scrapy's Request objects.

Unfortunately, we need some more configuration in the code of the scraper too. If you don't believe me, just start the scraper without having Splash running.

To get our scraper running through Splash, we need to adapt every request call to use a `SplashRequest`, and every time we initiate a new request (either when starting the scraper or `yield`-ing some `response. follow` calls).

To get the first start right, we can add the following function to our script:

```
from scrapy_splash import SplashRequest

def start_requests(self):
    for url in self.start_urls:
        yield SplashRequest(url, callback=self.parse)
```

This is the bare minimum to get the spider operating through Splash. The parameters speak for themselves: URL is the target URL, and `callback` defines the method to use. There are some options to configure how Splash should behave, for example, waiting some time to get the website rendered. Say, if we want to wait one second for loading the page, we can alter the calls of `SplashRequests` like this:

```
yield SplashRequest(url, callback=self.parse,
args={'wait':1.0})
```

So, we're good and we render the first page through Splash, but what about the other calls like navigating to the detail pages or the next page?

To adapt these, I changed the XPath extraction code a bit. Until now, we used the `response.follow` approach where we could provide the selector containing the potential next URL we want to scrape.

Using Splash, we need to extract these URLs and provide them as parameters to the `SplashRequest` constructor. I'll use the `parse` method as an example. It looked like this at the end of Chapter 4:

```
def parse(self, response):
    urls = response.xpath('//ul[@class="categories
    departments"]/li/a')
```

```
    for url in urls:
        yield response.follow(url, callback=self.parse_
        department_pages)
```

Now it looks like this:

```
def parse(self, response):
    urls = response.xpath('//ul[@class="categories
    departments"]/li/a/@href').extract()

    for url in urls:
        if url.startswith('http'):
            yield SplashRequest(url, callback=self.parse_
            department_pages)
```

I added the filter for url.startswith('http') to avoid potential errors that may happen if the url doesn't contain an absolute URL. In some cases, you need to join the URL together with the base URL of the response to get the target domain (because url is a relative URL to the domain). Following is an example again with the parse method.

```
def parse(self, response):
    urls = response.xpath('//ul[@class="categories
    departments"]/li/a/@href').extract()

    for url in urls:
        yield SplashRequest(response.urljoin(url),
        callback=self.parse_department_pages)
```

One change I made besides the ones mentioned previously was to rename the spider to splash.

Running the scraper stays the same.

```
scrapy crawl splash -o splashburys.jl
```

After the scraper finishes, you will find records similar to the following excerpt in the splashburys.jl file.

{"url": "https://www.sainsburys.co.uk/shop/ProductDisplay
?storeId=10151&productId=1153156&urlRequestType=Base&cate
goryId=312365&catalogId=10216&langId=44", "product_name":
"Sainsbury's Venison Steak, Taste the Difference 250g",
"product_image": "https://www.sainsburys.co.uk/wcsstore7.25.53/
ExtendedSitesCatalogAssetStore/images/catalog/productImages
/90/0000001442090/0000001442090_L.jpeg", "price_per_unit":
"£7.50", "rating": "3.0", "product_reviews": "2", "item_code":
"6450995", "nutritions": {"Energy ": "583kJ/", "Fat ": "2.6g",
"of which saturates ": "0.9g", "mono-unsaturates ": "1.0g",
"polyunsaturates ": "0.6g", "Carbohydrate ": "<0.5g", "of which
sugars ": "<0.5g", "Fibre ": "<0.5g", "Protein ": "28.2g",
"Sodium ": "0.05g", "Salt ": "0.13g"}, "product_origin": ""}
{"url": "https://www.sainsburys.co.uk/shop/gb/groceries/
special-offers-314361-44/sainsburys-salmon-with-lemon-butter-
-taste-the-difference-145g", "product_name": "Sainsbury's
Lightly Smoked Salmon with Wild Garlic Butter, Taste the
Difference 145g", "product_image": "https://www.sainsburys.
co.uk/wcsstore7.25.53/ExtendedSitesCatalogAssetStore/images/
catalog/productImages/27/0000000301527/0000000301527_L.jpeg",
"price_per_unit": "£3.00", "rating": "2.3333", "product_
reviews": "3", "item_code": "7880107", "nutritions": {"Energy":
"990kJ", "Energy kcal": "238kcal", "Fat": "16.9g", "Saturates":
"4.6g", "Mono-unsaturates": "7.5g", "Polyunsaturates": "3.8g",
"Carbohydrate": "1.6g", "Sugars": "1.2g", "Fibre": "0.6g",
"Protein": "19.6g", "Salt": "0.63g"}, "product_origin": "Packed
in United Kingdom Farmed in Scotland Produced from Farmed
Scottish (UK) Atlantic Salmon (Salmo salar)"}

And that is it: we converted the Sainsbury's scraper to use Splash.

What Happens When Splash Isn't Running?

Good question, but I bet you already have the answer. The scraper won't do anything, and exits with an error message containing the following valuable information to identify this particular error cause.

```
2018-04-27 16:07:19 [scrapy.core.scraper] ERROR: Error
downloading <GET https://www.sainsburys.co.uk/shop/gb/
groceries/meat-fish/ via http://localhost:8050/render.html>:
Connection was refused by other side: 10061:
```

Summary

Splash is a nice Python-based website rendering tool that you can integrate easily with Scrapy.

One drawback is that you must install it manually through a somewhat complicated process or using Docker. This makes porting it to the cloud complicated (see Chapter 6 for Cloud solutions), therefore you should use Splash only for a local scraper. However, locally it can give you a great benefit with its seamless integration with Scrapy for scraping websites using JavaScript to render content dynamically.

Another drawback is the speed. When I used Splash on my local computer, it barely scraped 20 pages per minute. This is too slow for my taste, but sometimes I cannot get around it.

Selenium

If you search the Internet about website scraping, you will most often encounter articles and questions about Selenium. Originally, I wanted to leave Selenium out of this book because I don't like its approach; it's a bit clumsy for my taste. However, because of its popularity, I decided to add a section about this tool. Perhaps you will embed a Selenium-based solution to your Scrapy scripts (for example you already have a Selenium-scraper but want to extend it), and I want to help you with this task.

First we will look at Selenium and how to use it in a stand-alone fashion, then we will add it to a Scrapy spider.

Prerequisites

To have Selenium working on your computer, you must install it like most Python libraries through the Python Package Index.

```
pip install selenium
```

To use Selenium for website scraping, you will need a web browser. This means you will see the configured web browser (let's say Firefox or Chrome) open up, load the website, and then Selenium does its work and extracts the script you defined.

To enable linking between Selenium and your browser, you must install a specific WebDriver.

For Chrome, visit https://sites.google.com/a/chromium.org/chromedriver/home. I downloaded version 2.38.

For Firefox, you need to install GeckoDriver. It can be found at GitHub. I downloaded version 0.20.1.

These drivers must be on the PATH when you're running your Python script. I put all of them inside a folder, because in this case I have to add only this one folder and all my web drivers are available.

Note   that these web drivers require a specific browser version. For example, if you already have Chrome installed and download the latest version of the web driver, you may encounter an exception like the one following if you miss updating your browser:

```
raise exception_class(message, screen, stacktrace)
selenium.common.exceptions.SessionNotCreatedException:
Message: session not created exception: Chrome version
must be >= 65.0.3325.0
```

```
(Driver info: chromedriver=2.38.552522 (437e6fbedfa
8762dec75e2c5b3ddb86763dc9dcb),platform=Windows NT
10.0.16299 x86_64)
```

Basic Usage

Now to verify if everything is working fine, let's write a simple script to open the Sainsbury's website for us using Selenium.

```
from selenium.webdriver import Chrome, Firefox

chrome = Chrome()
firefox = Firefox()

chrome.open()  # this opens a Chrome window
firefox.open()  # this opens a Firefox window

chrome.get('https://sainsburys.co.uk')  # navigates to the
target website in Chrome
firefox.get('https://sainsburys.co.uk')  # navigates to the
target website in Firefox
```

OK, it's nice to have the browser open automatically and navigate to the target website. But what about scraping information?

Because we have a website in our reach (in the browser), we can parse the HTML–almost like we did in the previous chapters or use Selenium's offering for data extraction from the HTML of the web page.

I won't go into detail on Selenium's extractors because it would exceed the boundaries of this book, but let me tell you that by using Selenium you have access to a different set of extraction functions, which you can use on your browser instances.

Integration with Scrapy

Selenium can be integrated with Scrapy. The only thing you need is to configure Selenium properly (have the web drivers on the PATH and the browsers installed) and then the fun can begin.

What I like to do is to disable the browser window for my scrapes. That's because I get distracted every time I see a browser window if it navigates the pages automatically, and it would go crazy if you combine Scrapy with Selenium.

Besides this, you will need a middleware that will intercept calls prior to sending them directly through Scrapy and will use Selenium instead of normal requests.

A rudimentary middleware would look like this one:

```python
# -*- coding: utf-8 -*-

from scrapy import signals
from scrapy.http import HtmlResponse
from scrapy.utils.python import to_bytes
from selenium import webdriver
from selenium.webdriver.firefox.options import Options

class SeleniumDownloaderMiddleware:

    def __init__(self):
        self.driver = None

    @classmethod
    def from_crawler(cls, crawler):
        middleware = cls()
        crawler.signals.connect(middleware.spider_opened,
        signals.spider_opened)
        crawler.signals.connect(middleware.spider_closed,
        signals.spider_closed)
        return middleware
```

```python
def process_request(self, request, spider):
    self.driver.get(request.url)
    body = to_bytes(self.driver.page_source)
    return HtmlResponse(self.driver.current_url, body=body,
    encoding='utf-8', request=request)

def spider_opened(self, spider):
    options = Options()
    options.set_headless()
    self.driver = webdriver.Firefox(options=options)

def spider_closed(self, spider):
    if self.driver:
        self.driver.close()
        self.driver.quit()
        self.driver = None
```

The preceding code uses Firefox as the default browser and starts it in headless mode when the spider is opened. When the spider closes, the web driver is closed too.

The interesting part is when the request happens: it is intercepted and routed through the browser and the response HTML code is wrapped into an HtmlResponse object. Now your spider gets the Selenium-loaded HTML code and you can use it for scraping.

scrapy-selenium

Recently, I have found a fresh project at GitHub called scrapy-selenium.[2] It is a convenient project to have you install and use it to combine the powers of Scrapy and Selenium. I think it is worth sharing this project with you.

---

[2]https://github.com/clemfromspace/scrapy-selenium

> **Note**   Because this project is a private one, it may have issues. If
> you find something not working, feel free to raise an issue for this
> project and the developer will help you out to fix that problem. If not,
> shoot me an email and I'll see if I can give you a solution or perhaps
> maintain the application myself and deliver newer versions.

This project works just like the custom middleware we implemented in the previous section: it intercepts requests and downloads the pages using Selenium.

Let's start with the configuration.

```
from shutil import which

SELENIUM_DRIVER_NAME = 'firefox'
SELENIUM_DRIVER_EXECUTABLE_PATH = which('geckodriver')
SELENIUM_DRIVER_ARGUMENTS = ['-headless']
```

Alternatively, you can use Chrome instead of Firefox, but in this case take care of the --headless argument: it requires two dashes.

```
from shutil import which

SELENIUM_DRIVER_NAME = 'chrome'
SELENIUM_DRIVER_EXECUTABLE_PATH = which('geckodriver')
SELENIUM_DRIVER_ARGUMENTS = ['--headless']
And we need the right middleware:
DOWNLOADER_MIDDLEWARES = {
    'scrapy_selenium.SeleniumMiddleware': 800
}
```

For the spider, I reused the code of the Splash section but changed the used Request implementation to the scrapy-selenium one:

```
from scrapy_selenium import SeleniumRequest
```

and I had to adapt the constructor calls to contain the URL as a named parameter.

```
def start_requests(self):
    for url in self.start_urls:
        yield SeleniumRequest(url=url, callback=self.parse)
```

Be sure you change all these calls. If you miss one, you'll get an error like this:

```
yield SeleniumRequest(url, callback=self.parse)
File "c:\dev\__py_venv\scrapy\lib\site-packages\scrapy_
selenium\http.py", line 29, in __init__
    super().__init__(*args, **kwargs)
TypeError: __init__() missing 1 required positional argument:
'url'
```

Summary

Selenium is an alternative tool that website scraper developers use because it supports JavaScript rendering through a browser. We saw some solutions on how to integrate Selenium with Scrapy but skipped the built-in methods to extract information.

Again, using an external tool like Selenium makes your scraping slower, even in headless mode.

Solutions for Beautiful Soup

Until now, we looked at solutions where we can integrate JavaScript-based website scraping with Scrapy. But some projects are fine using Beautiful Soup and don't need a full scraper environment.

Splash

Splash offers manual usage too. This means, you have an alternative option to get Splash to render a website and return the source code back to your code. And we can utilize this to have a simple scraper written with Beautiful Soup.

The idea here is to send an HTTP request to Splash, providing the URL to render (and any configuration parameters) and get the result back, and then use Beautiful Soup on this result, which is a rendered HTML.

To stick with the previous example, we will convert the scraper form Chapter 3 into a tool that utilizes Splash to render the pages of Sainsbury's.

The idea here is to simply call Splash's HTTP API to render the web page instead of getting the page through the requests library. This means our only change will be in the get_page function, where we forward the URL we want to scrape to Splash.

```
def get_page(url):
    try:
        r = requests.get('http://localhost:8050/render.
        html?url=' + url)
        if r.status_code == 200:
            return BeautifulSoup(r.content, bs_parser)
    except Exception as e:
        pass
    return None
```

As you can see, we call the render.html endpoint of our Splash installation and provide the target URL as a simple GET parameter.

If you're more into POST requests, you can change the prceding function to look like this:

```
def get_page(url):
    try:
        r = requests.post('http://localhost:8050/render.html',
        data='{'url': '+ url + '}')
```

```
        if r.status_code == 200:
            return BeautifulSoup(r.content, bs_parser)
    except Exception as e:
        pass
    return None
```

Selenium

Of course, we can integrate Selenium to our Beautiful Soup solutions too. It works the same way as it did with Scrapy.

Again, I won't use the built-in Selenium methods to extract information from the website. I use Selenium only to render the page and extract the information I require.

To do this, I'll add two helper functions to the scraper, which initialize and tear down Selenium at the required places.

```
def initialize():
    global selenium
    if not selenium:
        selenium = Firefox()

def tear_down():
    global selenium
    if selenium:
        selenium.quit()
        selenium = None
```

To be on the safe side, I'll add a call to initialize() every time we want to download a page; however, I'll call tear_down() only when the script finishes.

```
def get_page(url):
    initialize()
```

```
try:
    selenium.get(url)
    return BeautifulSoup(selenium.page_source, bs_parser)
except Exception as e:
    pass
return None
```

Summary

Even though we focus on Scrapy, because in my opinion it's currently **the website scraping tool for Python**, you can see that options that make Scrapy handle JavaScript can be added to "plain" Beautiful Soup scrapers. And this gives you options to stay with the tools you already know!

Summary

In this chapter we looked at some approaches to scrape websites that utilize JavaScript. We looked at the mainstream Selenium using a web browser to execute JavaScript and then went to the headless world, where you don't need any window to execute JavaScript and this makes your scripts portable and easier to execute.

Naturally, using another tool to get some extra rendering done takes time and provides overhead. If you don't require JavaScript rendering, create your scripts without any add-ons like Splash or Selenium. You'll benefit from the speed gain.

Now we are ready to see how we can deploy our spiders to the Cloud!

CHAPTER 6

Website Scraping in the Cloud

Running website scraping locally is fine for do-once tasks and small amounts of data, where you can easily trigger the crawl manually.

However, if you want reoccurring tasks and automatic scheduling, you should think about other solutions such as deploying your spiders somewhere into the cloud or a bought server slot.

In this chapter we will look at the virtual network of servers, the cloud, and what options you have if you want to use website scraping in the cloud. I'll focus on Scrapy because it is the tool for website scraping and there are services provided and matched for use with Scrapy.

Scrapy Cloud

The name tells you everything: Scrapy Cloud[1] is a cloud solution where you can deploy your Scrapy spiders. As the website states: "Think of it as a Heroku for web crawling."

---

[1]`https://scrapinghub.com/scrapy-cloud`

© Gábor László Hajba 2018
G. L. Hajba, *Website Scraping with Python*, https://doi.org/10.1007/978-1-4842-3925-4_6

Creating a Project

When you arrive at ScrapingHub, you will want to create a project because the page you get is empty, as shown in Figure 6-1.

Figure 6-1. My company's empty ScrapingHub overview

Fortunately, it is intuitive: we must click the green button in the upper right corner.

We will use Scrapy spiders, so select this option, as shown in Figure 6-2.

Figure 6-2. Creating a new project

Now that the project is created, we must upload our spider to the cloud. There are two options: over the command line or cloning a GitHub repository, as you can see in Figure 6-3. We will go with the command line solution because I am a nerd, and because most of the time I use some internal Git system and not GitHub to store my code.

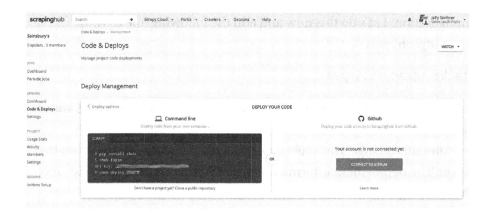

Figure 6-3. *New project and upload options*

If you decide to use the command line, you have two options: to deploy directly or a Docker image. I will stay with the simple deploy version for now.

Deploying Your Spider

Because I use the basic command line deployment, I go to the spider's base folder (where the `scrapy.cfg` file is located) and execute the following commands:

```
pip install shub
shub login
shub deploy
```

After you run the `shub deploy` command the first time, you will see following message among others:

```
Saved to scrapinghub\sainsburys\scrapinghub.yml.
```

This file is important because you must edit this file if you deploy a Python 3 spider. And because I focused on Python 3, we will use this configuration. Let's do this now and add the following line to your `scrapinghub.yml`:

```
stack: scrapy:1.5-py3
```

This tells ScrapingHub that you want to use Scrapy version `1.5` running in a Python 3 environment.

After this change, run `shub deploy` again to update the spider on the server. The deployment information is then something similar to what is shown in Figure 6-4.

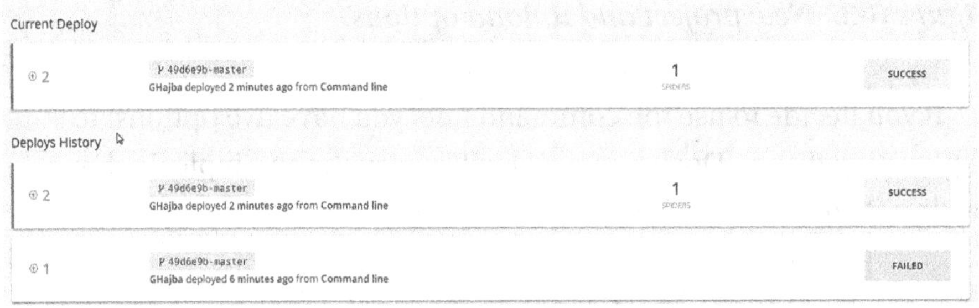

Figure 6-4. Deployment info and history

Start and Wait

After deployment, in the upper left corner you will see that you have one spider, like in Figure 6-5. Clicking this link (or the `Dashboard` menu entry in the Spiders section) navigates you to your spiders.

Figure 6-5. *Spiders in the project*

Clicking the basic spider (for me the only spider deployed) will get you to the spider's page, as shown in Figure 6-6. Here you can change some project specific settings, and you can run the spider.

Figure 6-6. *Spider details*

Running the Sainsbury's spider takes some time. But you can do it and wait for its completion. After running the spiders, you will see all information about runs–even if you had errors while running your spiders, as shown in Figure 6-7.

Figure 6-7. *Completed jobs*

As you can see, you get information about loaded items, sent requests, and some statistics. If you click the job's number, you will get some detailed statistics and you can look at the items extracted by the run, as shown in Figure 6-8.

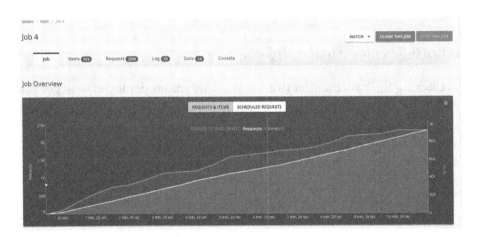

Figure 6-8. *Some basic statistics of the run*

Accessing the Data

You can access the extracted information in some ways. The most common access is to download your results in some format, as you would export it while running Scrapy from your command line, as shown in Figure 6-9.

Figure 6-9. *Export options*

As you can see, you get some options and one will fit your project's needs.

An alternative option is to publish your dataset. This makes it available to people even without knowing how you gathered the data. Publishing comes in three flavors:

- *Public*: Everyone has access to the data, no need for ScrapingHub account, and search engines can index it.

- *Protected*: Only users with ScrapingHub account can access this data.

- *Private*: Oonly members of your ScrapingHub organization can access the data.

If you have confident information, then use private. ScrapingHub has some issues with publicly available datasets, and you cannot access them without a ScrapingHub account.

Anyhow, if you want to publish a dataset, you must provide a description and a logo to it to be publicly available. I agree with the description, but a logo is in my eyes too much. Sure, if you look at the catalog,[2] you will see why a logo is required, as shown in Figure 6-10.

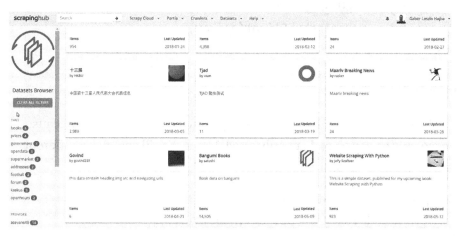

Figure 6-10. *The public dataset catalog*

---

[2]https://app.scrapinghub.com/datasets

From these datasets, you can download the items the same way you can through your job's page. Note, that you have to be logged in to see the available datasets.

API

ScrapingHub provides an API that you can use to access your data programmatically. Let's examine this option too.

I suggest you use the scrapinghub Python library, because accessing the API directly (with curl for example) doesn't work the way it is described in the documentation.

```
pip install scrapinghub[msgpack]
```

Now we're ready to access our data from a simple Python code. I'll use the interactive interpreter so you can follow along.

```
>>> from scrapinghub import ScrapinghubClient
>>> apikey = 'YOUR-API-KEY'
>>> client = ScrapinghubClient(apikey)
>>>
>>> client.projects.list()
[310577]
```

The first step, after logging in, is to get the ID of our project. Because I have only one project, I get only one ID back. You'll get back a different one, so replace accordingly.

```
>>> project = client.get_project(310577)
>>> [j['key'] for j in project.jobs.list()]
['310577/1/4']
```

Above we list all the jobs associated with the project. This job key is needed to access the data. If you have long-running jobs, you can use the state flag of the job's metadata information:

```
>>> job = project.jobs.get('310577/1/4')
>>> job.metadata.get('state')
'finished'
```

Now that we have the job we're interested in, let's retrieve all the items.

```
>>> job.items.iter()
<generator object mpdecode at 0x000001DAC5092D58>
>>> for item in job.items.iter(count=1):
...     print(item)
...
{'url': 'https://www.sainsburys.co.uk/shop/ProductDisplay
?storeId=10151&productId=1219376&urlRequestType=Base&cate
goryId=275324&catalogId=10100&langId=44', 'product_name':
"Sainsbury's British Pork Mince 20% Fat 500g", 'product_
image': 'https://www.sainsburys.co.uk/wcsstore7.27.110/
ExtendedSitesCatalogAssetStore/images/catalog/productI
mages/93/0000000327893/0000000327893_L.jpeg', 'image_
urls': ['https://www.sainsburys.co.uk/wcsstore7.27.110/
ExtendedSitesCatalogAssetStore/images/catalog/productImages
/93/0000000327893/0000000327893_L.jpeg'], 'price_per_unit':
'£1.65', 'rating': '0.0', 'product_reviews': '0', 'item_
code': '7916164', 'nutritions': {'Energy kJ': '1104', 'Energy
kcal': '265', 'Fat': '18.9g', 'of which saturates': '6.5g',
'- mono-unsaturates': '8.0g', '- polyunsaturates': '3.5g',
'Carbohydrate': '1.0g', 'of which sugars': '<0.5g', 'Fibre':
'0.6g', 'Protein': '22.5g', 'Salt': '0.50g'}, 'product_origin': ",
'_type': 'SainsburysItem'}
```

As you can see in the preceding code, you can get a generator over the items associated with the job; I printed out the first result of the list. If you're interested in how many items have been extracted, you can use the metadata of the job again.

```
>>> job.metadata.get('scrapystats')['item_scraped_count']
923
```

As you can see, the API is very useful to split up data extraction from websites and process them automatically with scripts later.

Limitations

Free accounts have some limitations. Let's look at them, even if you can go along very well with these limits.

First, there is a limitation of **one concurrent crawl**, which means you can only run one spider at a time. For starting out, this is not a problem because you will rarely want to run spiders in parallel. If the number of your customers is growing, then you can encounter occasions when you need parallel runs to gather data faster.

The second limitation, which can be annoying if you have jobs that should be run frequently, is **no periodic jobs**. You can configure them, but they won't run until you subscribe to a paid plan, which start currently at $9 per month.

The third big limitation is **data storage**. Your scraped results are stored only for seven days. After that time, your crawl result is history. You can extend this period to 120 days if you subscribe to a paid plan. But you can overcome this problem if you have automatic data processing (through the API), or if you store your data in a database.

Summary

ScrapingHub is the ideal solution in my eyes, if you have bigger Scrapy projects, because it offers an easy to use platform for setting up and evaluating your project. The presence of the Python library to access your scraped data (and interacting with your spiders too) makes it convenient both to automate data extraction and work with this data. The free plan gives you a lot, and help is there to get you started.

PythonAnywhere

OK, there are other options besides ScrapingHub, of course. One is PythonAnywhere,[3] a platform solution that enables you to run Python in the cloud. It has a free "beginner" account, which has limitations on outbound internet access, CPU, and memory usage, but it will fit our purposes.

In this section we will create a simple scraper written in Scrapy, and we will upload it to the cloud.

The Example Script

We will use a different Scrapy script, because the free account has limitations on websites that you can reach from your scripts and Sainsbury's is not listed.

Therefore, I picked a website and created a simple scraper that will extract the name and the description of the sights and attractions in Berlin.

---

[3]https://www.pythonanywhere.com/

PythonAnywhere Configuration

Now it's time to configure our PythonAnywhere account and get the script in the cloud. I'll give you a step-by-step description here for the current version of the PythonAnywhere solution–as it is on the **3rd April 2018**.

Install Scrapy with the following command:

```
pip install --user scrapy
```

The --user flag is required because you are not allowed to modify the global Python package installations, and you cannot ad Scrapy to it either.

Now we have everything set up for our scraper. To verify this, you can execute the following command:

```
~ $ scrapy version
Scrapy 1.5.0
```

Well, installing Scrapy and all its dependencies consumes the daily assigned CPU capacity. If you want to continue with this chapter's examples, you can, but it can get slow on a free PythonAnywhere account.

Uploading the Script

There are some ways to get your scripts up to PythonAnywhere:

- cloning from Github / BitBucket

- uploading as a ZIP file (actually, you can upload it file-by-file, but ZIP is more convenient)

- SFTP and Rsync for paying accounts

I used the ZIP approach: compressed the Scrapy project; uploaded it from the "Files" menu in PythonAnywhere; and then uncompressed it using the unzip command, as shown in Figures 6-11 and 6-12.

Figure 6-11. *The* berlin.zip *file is uploaded into my home folder*

```
         Bash console 8556505
10:46 ~ $ unzip berlin
Archive:  berlin.zip
   creating: berlin/
   creating: berlin/berlin/
  inflating: berlin/berlin/items.py
  inflating: berlin/berlin/middlewares.py
  inflating: berlin/berlin/pipelines.py
  inflating: berlin/berlin/settings.py
   creating: berlin/berlin/spiders/
  inflating: berlin/berlin/spiders/sights.py
  inflating: berlin/berlin/spiders/__init__.py
   creating: berlin/berlin/spiders/__pycache__/
  inflating: berlin/berlin/spiders/__pycache__/sights.cpython-36.pyc
  inflating: berlin/berlin/spiders/__pycache__/__init__.cpython-36.pyc
 extracting: berlin/berlin/__init__.py
   creating: berlin/berlin/__pycache__/
  inflating: berlin/berlin/__pycache__/items.cpython-36.pyc
  inflating: berlin/berlin/__pycache__/pipelines.cpython-36.pyc
  inflating: berlin/berlin/__pycache__/settings.cpython-36.pyc
  inflating: berlin/berlin/__pycache__/__init__.cpython-36.pyc
  inflating: berlin/scrapy.cfg
10:46 ~ $
```

Figure 6-12. *Unzipping the package*

Now the folder is available under the *Files* section of the dashboard, as shown in Figure 6-13.

Figure 6-13. *The files containing the* `berlin` *folder*

Running the Script

Now we can run the script from our Bash console the same way as locally, as shown in Figure 6-14. And because we have a file system, we can export the results as files too. For example, to get the sights and attractions in a JSON-lines file, we can execute the following command:

```
scrapy crawl sights -o sights.jl
```

Figure 6-14. *Running the spider*

When the script finishes, like in Figure 6-15, a new file is written into the project's folder. If there's already a file, Scrapy will append the new information to it instead of recreating the file from scratch. Remember this!

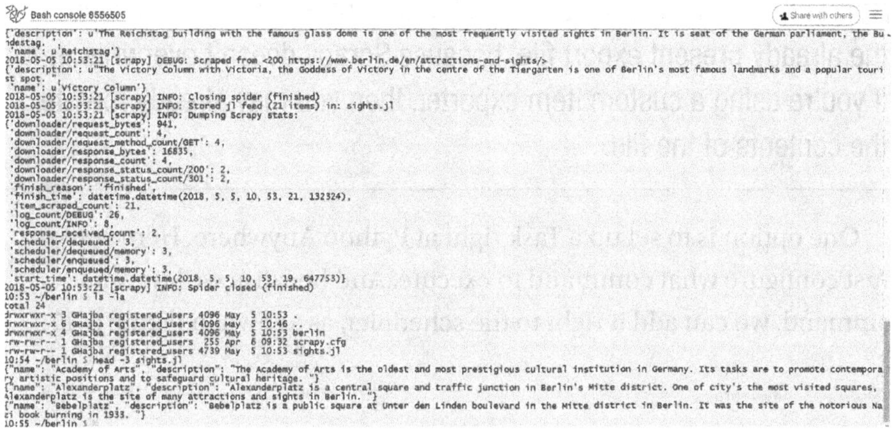

Figure 6-15. *Spider finished and the first three lines of the file*

You can access the file through the *Files* page. Here you can download the file, but it is possible to edit it in your browser, as shown in Figure 6-16.

Figure 6-16. *Download the exported file*

This Works Just Manually...

For now, we only ran the script manually. But this is not the way we sought when we deployed the scraper in the cloud.

The solution is to add a scheduler, which automatically starts the scraper at a defined time.

Remember   if you are using a scheduler, make sure you remove the already present export file, because Scrapy doesn't overwrite it. If you're using a custom item exporter, then you may already rewrite the contents of the file.

One option is to set up a Task right at Python Anywhere. Here you must configure what command to execute. And because we know our command, we can add it right to the scheduler, as shown in Figure 6-17.

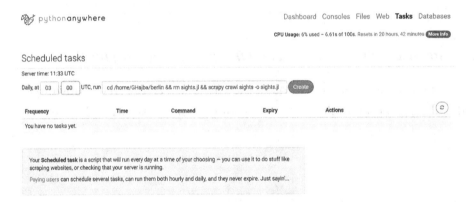

Figure 6-17. *Creating the task using a three-piece script*

After the scheduled time up, you have access to the task log that contains the console output, and perhaps some errors, as shown in Figure 6-18.

Figure 6-18. *Accessing the log for a task*

The second approach is the extended version of the previous one: we create a script that executes the command sequence defined earlier, and we point the scheduler to this script.

The first step is to create a script that changes to the project's folder and executes the spider (make sure, you're pointing to your home folder!).

```
#!/bin/bash
cd /home/GHajba/berlin
rm sights.jl
scrapy crawl sights -o sights.jl
```

The preceding script is the same we provided previously to the task, but we placed every command on its own line and this makes it readable.

I created the file right in my browser using PythonAnywhere's editor, as shown in Figure 6-19.

Figure 6-19. *Creating a new file*

Caveat   If you're using a Windows computer, the file editor will add Windows line-endings to your file. To fix this issue (and be able to run the script in a Bash shell) execute the following command from the console: `sed -i -e 's/\r$//' berlin_scheduler.sh`

Because a free account has limitations on the number of scheduled tasks (you can have only one), we will drop the previously created one and create a new one that will execute only the previously created `berlin_scheduler.sh`, as shown in Figure 6-20.

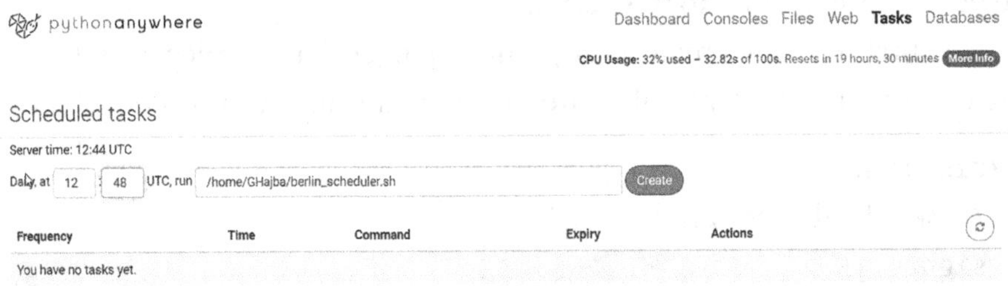

Figure 6-20. *Creating the new scheduler*

After the task is available, you have access to the task log, which contains the same information as previously.

Storing Data in a Database?

It would be a viable option to store the extracted results in a database. Because we're in the cloud and using PythonAnywhere for now, it would be ideal to have cloud storage–for example, mLab, which is a cloud-based MongoDB.

The problem is that a free account allows only HTTP and HTTPS connections to servers. This means, even though you set-up a Mongo database with mLab, you cannot create a connection to store the data.

However, Python Anywhere offers MySQL for free users. This means, you can have storage for your extracted information, and you don't have to store everything in a file.

Let's look at how to configure MySQL and store the extracted data in the database.

First, let's create a database. You can do this on the *Databases*. I named mine `berlinsights`, as shown in Figure 6-21.

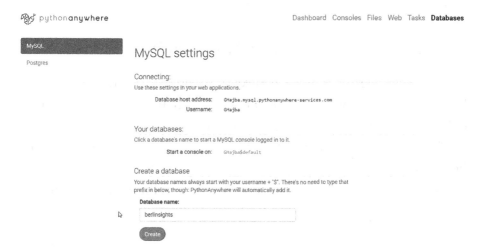

Figure 6-21. *Creating a new database is easy*

Now we must configure our Scrapy project to be able to connect to the database and write information to the given table.

We will use a simple item pipeline that will insert the sights into the database.

And we need the database table. I created it through the database console using the following script:

```
create table berlinsights( name varchar(1024) not null,
description varchar(4096));
```

```
MySQL: GHajba$berlinsights

Welcome to the MySQL monitor.  Commands end with ; or \g.
Your MySQL connection id is 16622989
Server version: 5.6.27-log MySQL Community Server (GPL)

Copyright (c) 2000, 2016, Oracle and/or its affiliates. All rights reserved.

Oracle is a registered trademark of Oracle Corporation and/or its
affiliates. Other names may be trademarks of their respective
owners.

Type 'help;' or '\h' for help. Type '\c' to clear the current input statement.

mysql> use GHajba$berlinsights
Database changed
mysql> create table berlinsights( name varchar(1024) not null, description varchar(4096));
Query OK, 0 rows affected (0.04 sec)

mysql>
```

Figure 6-22. *Creating the table using the console*

As you can see in Figure 6-22: make sure, you're using the right database! If you're not sure which database you're running on, type status and it will tell you which database you're on.

If you forget your database password, you can simply set a new one at the database dashboard.

Now we can create our middleware. We will use the pymysql library.

```
# -*- coding: utf-8 -*-

import pymysql.cursors

insert_template = """INSERT INTO berlinsights (name,
description) VALUES (%s, %s)"""

class BerlinMySQLPipeline(object):

    def process_item(self, item, spider):
        connection = pymysql.connect(host='GHajba.mysql.
        pythonanywhere-services.com',
                                     user='GHajba',
                                     password='YourDbPassHere',
                                     db='GHajba$berlinsights',
                                     charset='utf8mb4',
```

```
                          cursorclass=pymysql.cursors.
                          DictCursor)
    try:
        with connection.cursor() as cursor:
            cursor.execute(insert_template, (item['name'],
            item['description']))
            connection.commit()
    finally:
        connection.close()

    return item
```

The prceding example uses my database, so make sure you're filling in your data! And because this MySQL database is a PythonAnywhere service, you can test your connection only when you've deployed your scraper.

Again, this script doesn't validate if an entry is already in the database. If you run it twice, you will get every entry duplicated. Feel free to adapt the script to filter or update already present entries.

After running the spider, we can verify that information is in the database, as shown in Figure 6-23.

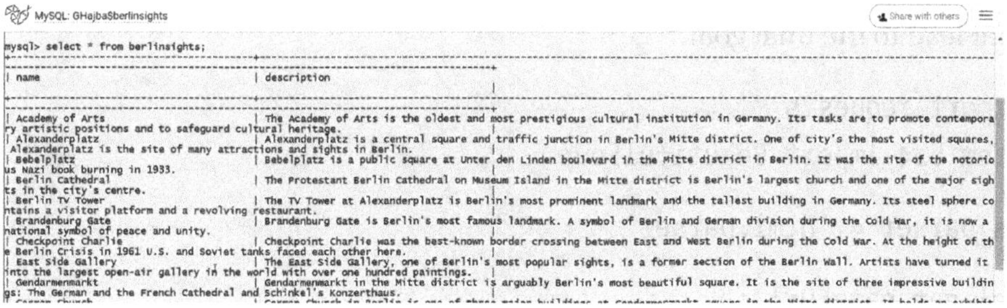

Figure 6-23. *Verifying the data in the console*

If didn't installed pymysql already, you can do it with the following command:

```
pip install --user pymysq
```

Summary

Python Anywhere offers you cloud hosting and scheduling for free; however, it has limitations on the outgoing connections for the free plan. And this makes it only valuable for practicing. On the other side, if you pay $5 a month, you get an upgraded account where you don't have to limit your scrapings to the whitelist.[4]

What About `Beautiful Soup`?

PythonAnywhere is a cloud platform for Python. This means you can not only run Scrapy spiders there but `Beautiful Soup` scrapers too. And this is what we will look at in a nutshell.

The approach is the same as previously: we will extract the same sights but using Beautiful Soup.

Fortunately, the `requests` and `beautifulsoup4` libraries are already installed on the host computer, so you do not need to install anything.

The first step is to write and upload the script. Actually, I have already written the code, but this doesn't mean you cannot do it for yourself. As always: my code examples are just **one solution** and there are many paths that lead to the final goal.

```
import requests
from bs4 import BeautifulSoup

bs_parser = 'html.parser'

def get_page(url):
    try:
        r = requests.get(url)
        if r.status_code == 200:
```

---

[4]https://www.pythonanywhere.com/whitelist/

```
            return BeautifulSoup(r.content, bs_parser)
    except Exception as e:
        pass
    return None

def get_sights():
    soup = get_page('https://www.berlin.de/en/attractions-and-
    sights/')
    if not soup:
        return

    for sight in soup.select('div[class*="teaser"]'):
        h3 = sight.find('h3')
        if not h3:
            continue
        a = h3.find('a')
        if not a:
            continue
        name = a.text
        if not name:
            continue

        description = "
        div = sight.find('div', class_='inner')
        if div:
            p = div.find('p')
            if p:
                description = p.text
        if not description:
            continue
        yield (name, description)
```

```
if __name__ == '__main__':
    with open('berlin_sights.jl', 'w') as outfile:
        for sight in get_sights():
            outfile.write('{' + '"name": "{}", "description":
            "{}"'.format(sight[0], sight[1]) + '}\n')
```

After uploading, we can run the script. Running the script works as it would in a normal terminal window.

```
python3 berlin.py
```

After the process finishes, you can access the results in the `berlin_sights.jl` file. The first entry looks like this:

```
{"name": "Academy of Arts", "description": "The Academy of
Arts is the oldest and most prestigious cultural institution
in Germany. Its tasks are to promote contemporary artistic
positions and to safeguard cultural heritage. more »"}
```

Scheduling a script works the same way it did for Scrapy scripts, so I won't go into detail. Think of PythonAnywhere as your remote Python terminal if you're using `Beautiful Soup`.

Summary

In this chapter we looked at options for how to run scrapers in the cloud. This is the solution if you don't want to run your extractors every time manually, or you don't want to have them run on your computer because they eat a lot of resources and your computer gets slow for a long time.

We looked at Scraping Hub, which provides services specific for `Scrapy` and this makes it unique. Besides this, they're the developers of Splash too and they have a solution for how you can run your Splash-based spiders in the cloud.

As an alternative, we looked at PythonAnywhere, where you can upload Python scripts and execute them. This is not only useful for `Scrapy` but for scripts using Beautiful Soup too, and this moves your simple scrapers into the Cloud too.

Index

A

Autothrottling, 165–166

B

Beautiful Soup, 4, 12
  with scrapy, 161
  Selenium, 191–192
  Splash, 190–191
Beautiful Soup scrapers, 214–216
  converting Soup to
    HTML text, 53
  to CSV (*see* CSV module)
  developing long run
    cache intermediate step
      results, 90
    database cache, 92
    file-based cache, 92
    saving space, 93
    updating cache, 94
  exporting data
    JSON files, 73–75
    NoSQL database, 83–85
    relational database, 76–82
    saving class, 70–73
    saving dictionary, 69–70
  extracting all images, 46
  extracting all links, 45–46
  extracting required
    information, 53
  navigating product
    pages, 56–57
  target URLs, 54–56
  using classes, 62
  using dictionaries, 58–62
  find and find_all, 45
  finding comments, 52
  finding tags on property, 48
  finding tags through
    attributes, 46–47
  installing, 41
  nutrition table, 63–64
  parsing file, 45
  parsing HTML text, 42–43
  parsing remote HTML, 44
  performance improvements
    changing parser, 86
    parse only needed, 87–88
    saving while working, 88–89
  source code, 95
  tags and attributes
    adding, 49–50
    changing, 50–51
    deleting, 51
  unforeseen changes, 63–64
Breadth First Search (BFS), 56
builtwith library, 7–8

Printed in the United States
By Bookmasters